DODGING FATE

A CHARLIE KENNY REDSHIRT ADVENTURE

ZEN DIPIETRO

PARALLEL WORLDS PRESS

COPYRIGHT © 2018 BY ZEN DIPIETRO

This is a work of fiction. Names, characters, organizations, events, and incidents are either products of the author's imagination or used fictitiously. Any resemblance to actual events, business establishments, locales, or persons, living or dead, is coincidental.

All rights reserved. No part of this publication may be reproduced, stored in a retrieval system, or transmitted in any form or by any means (electronic, mechanical, photocopying, recording, or otherwise) without express written permission of the publisher. The only exception is brief quotations for the purpose of review.

Please purchase only authorized electronic editions. Distribution of this book via the Internet or via any other means without the permission of the publisher is illegal and punishable by law.

ISBN: 978-1-943931-27-9 (print)

Cover Art by Dyana Wangsa

Published in the United States of America by Parallel Worlds Press

MESSAGE FROM THE AUTHOR

Thank you for reading!

If you enjoyed this book and can spare a minute or two to leave a review on Amazon, I'd be grateful. It makes a big difference.

Do you want to read more of Charlie, Greta, and Pinky? Dodging Fate 2 promises blagrook-whacking, adventure...and maybe even...love. You can check it out on Amazon.

Sign up for my newsletter at www.ZenDiPietro.com to hear about new releases and sales.

I hope to hear from you!

In gratitude,
Zen DiPietro

MY NAME IS CHARLIE KENNY, AND I'M A REDSHIRT

1

So, I'm a redshirt.

I come from a long line of redshirts. I denied it for a long time, but when your family members have a habit of getting decapitated, impaled, or just plain dematerialized, you eventually have to face facts.

My dad had his spine removed from his body when a member of his crew de-evolved into what I can only describe as a cross between an alligator and a yeti. A yeti-gator, as we now refer to it.

My uncle was bitten by a phase-shifted arachnid and unintentionally relocated to an alternative universe that didn't have oxygen. I mean, seriously. Try calculating those odds.

My grandmother was happily baking cookies when a cyborg transported into her kitchen and assimilated her. Technically, she's still alive, and she does send me cookies every now and then, but to be honest, they taste like shit. Cyborgs have no idea how to make proper cookies.

My great-grandfather had just landed a cargo ship full of rutabagas when a nearby ship malfunctioned and shot a harpoon straight into the cockpit. *A frigging harpoon.* It doesn't even make sense. You know what else? I have no idea what rutabagas are used for.

There are more examples, but relating the tragic demises of the majority of my family members is bumming me out. Do you have any idea how depressing family reunions are for the few of us that are left? So, let's move on.

As soon as I accepted that I'm a redshirt (thanks to the diligent psychotherapy provided by one Dr. Ramalama), I decided I would be the one to break the cycle. To stop the madness. To change my family for the better, in the hope that one day we can qualify for the group discount when we visit the buffet on Mars. I have dreams. (I'm not kidding, the hushpuppies there are to die for. If you ever go there, carry a really big purse. You'll thank me later.)

Also, not being terrified for my life every time I get onto an escalator would be great. People look at you like you're a real dumbass when you take a running leap to avoid the grates at the terminus. Besides, I have a cousin who died jumping. Just jumping. She landed, fractured both her femurs and suffered a pulmonary embolism. As a result, I kind of have a complex about jumping.

Actually, I have to be honest. I have a lot of complexes. I suspect Dr. Ramalama guided me toward my epiphany of self-realization just so I would leave the planet. Someone like me is just too much work for one mental healthcare professional. Whenever I brought up my fear of forks, I could practically hear her eyes roll.

That's how I got to this point: boarding a transport ship for Mebdar IV. It's a retirement planet. Most people see it as a fate worse than death. *"Don't even think of shipping me off to Mebdar IV,"* I've heard many an elderly person say. But when it's well established that your fate *is* death, your priorities shift. And for a guy like me, a place where all the food is soft with no bones or pits inside, and most walkways are lined with handrails, and there's always staff nearby to hear a call for help...well, it sounds like perfection.

But before I can settle myself into that bubble-wrapped, user-friendly existence, I have to make it to Mebdar IV. This means a lengthy trip among the stars and, I assure you, space travel has never been kind to my people. I'd say, "Just ask my dad," but you already know what happened to him. (The yeti-gator-spine-removal procedure.)

I can only hope my first trip into space will be less eventful.

2

My trip to the space port proves to be unremarkable, which gives me hope for the journey ahead, even as Dr. Ramalama's words ring in my memory. *"Charlie, your attempts to create order in the universe by watching for harbingers is irrational."*

I know it's true. But I also know that my cousin Tilda got a metal splinter in her finger from an ill-wrought writing scrib. She contracted blood poisoning almost immediately and died within a week. There are more ways to die than Dr. Ramalama ever thought about, and for me, forgetting about that fact would be the truly irrational action.

As my taxi pulls into the passenger drop-off lane and I get out, I carefully watch for veering vehicles, runaway luggage trolleys, and robots run amok. It doesn't matter that these events are unlikely. They happen, and when they do, you can bet I'm going to be right there, front and center, poised to become another redshirt headline.

As I enter the space port, I feel a small measure of relief, but I've only made it over one tiny hurdle. There are many more to come.

Don't even get me started on how many ways there are to die.

Dodging Fate

We poor bastards of squishy cellular composition, with our delicate throats and exposed eyeballs and need for a very specific mix of air are all but destined for a sad, messy end. It's like some sick sadist actually designed us for maximum suffering. We're just too high maintenance.

This is an advantage the cyborgs and AIs have over us. It's an advantage that, honestly, I sometimes covet. I mean, I could deal with only being able to make shitty cookies and having to be careful around strong magnets. But sacrificing my brain, autonomy, and greater consciousness is too high a price. Therefore, I'm stuck with this soft, vulnerable body, which is basically just a bag of water with a little carbon thrown in.

As I look at the throngs of people moving through the spaceport, I take a deep breath and begin my calming exercise. It's a technique Dr. Ramalama taught me where I focus on something that gives me a sense of control. In accordance with both my nature and my profession, I mentally calculate the probabilities of various events.

My background as a redshirt, along with my likelihood of a tragic and untimely end, prompted me to become a statistician. One of the first things you learn in statistics class is that a previous random event has no bearing at all on the next random event. But someone like Dr. Ramalama doesn't know what I know; that good luck and bad luck are as real as gravity or solar radiation.

Just because you can't see luck doesn't mean it isn't a true force of nature. The mechanics of it are the secret of the universe, but it's a genuine and measurable phenomenon.

I really need the universe to provide me with a little good luck to see me through this voyage. I knew this all along as I prepared for this trip, but as I step into the writhing mass of eager travelers, I feel my family legacy—my probable fate—in the back of my throat. Threatening to choke me.

People are rushing around me in all possible directions, often while carrying heavy baggage. I carry only one slim overnight bag. Having read about the muggings that can occur when a person is overburdened and distracted, I chose to send my belongings to Mebdar IV ahead of me. I don't mind wearing my single outfit and pair of pajamas every day. My manner of dress is consistent even when I have a full closet. A slim pair of beige trousers ensures that I don't get tripped up by excess fabric, while a plain beige stretch-knit shirt provides the most opportunity to escape from anything that might snag the garment. Nowhere on my person do I have hanging tabs, ties, or dangling pieces that might get slammed in a door, caught on a chair, or otherwise be turned into a way of strangling or hanging me.

I do not want my epitaph to read: *Here lies Charles Kenny. He was strangled by his own pants.* If I'm going to die in some terrible way, at least it should be something with some pizzazz, like Nana being assimilated into a cyborg.

I wonder how she is. I should write her a letter.

Carrying my bag in front of me, I carefully avoid making contact with the people hurrying by. I don't want to get beaten to a pulp for brushing shoulders with some macho Taklarian brute. I ignore the food cart vendors and their fantastic-smelling goods because I do not need food poisoning. Likewise, I hustle right by the gorgeous girls selling exotic vacations and unrealistic dreams. Not because I fear they might attack me in some way, but because, for a guy like me, a woman that beautiful is bound to be the death of me in some slower, subtler, and excruciatingly painful way.

I have to make a right turn just in front of one of these fantastic creatures. I pretend not to hear her siren song offering a free night's stay and complimentary bar pass for a week's vacation on the beaches of Faarklaar.

It's a prettier planet than the name implies.

Awash with relief and the unfamiliar feeling of success, I make it to the docking gate, and take a seat to wait. After ten minutes, the door to the gate opens and a smiling human of around fifty years arrives to welcome me and usher me to the airlock.

"Will this be your first visit to the Mebdar system?" he asks as he escorts me.

"Yes."

"Ah, well, I think you'll enjoy it. I hope you enjoy your voyage as well. Garbdorian starships aren't pretty, but their safety record is superior to that of any other fleet."

"Yes, that's why I chose this airline. That, and the fact that they staff their ships with people who speak a variety of languages. I didn't want a miscommunication to result in my grisly death."

The man seems taken aback. I may have said too much.

But he recovers quickly. "Well, no worries about that here. Our staff will speak to you in Earth Standard, if that's what you prefer."

"Yes. Thank you."

As I step into the airlock, he looks hesitant. "Though, I should warn you about the signs on the ship. The Garbdorians pride themselves on translating all languages into Standard and, well, sometimes they don't quite convey the intended message. Be sure to ask a staff member when in doubt."

That seemed less than promising, but it was too late to rethink my choices. "Okay. Thank you."

He brightens. "Enjoy your trip."

Enjoyment would be nice, but I'd happily settle for mere survival.

I CAREFULLY STEP over the ridge on the other side of the airlock. There's a one-millimeter difference between the ship side and the lock side. Most people wouldn't notice it, and certainly no one would ever trip on it. Unless that someone was me.

Once officially aboard the ship, I notice a sign that says, *Please careful your walking in vestigial parallel of conformity.*

As I try to figure that out, a dapper looking steward swoops in. "Welcome, Mr. Kenny. Thank you for choosing the *Second Chance* for your voyage. Please let us know if there's anything we can help you with."

"Hang on. This ship is named *Second Chance*?" My ticket only listed a Chance Fleet registry number.

"Yes, sir." The reed-thin man holds his hands in front of him, with his fingers forming a tent sort of shape.

"What happened to the *First Chance*? Did something go wrong?"

"Oh, no. The *Chance* is still flying. This is the second in the Chance Fleet. We have seven now, and hundreds of thousands of happy customers."

Explained that way, it doesn't seem so bad. I was worried there for a second.

I point to the puzzling sign. "What does that mean?"

"That's translated from Martian. It just means to watch your step, since some species are very sensitive to even the subtlest of changes in artificial gravity. The warning is mostly for Martians, who have unusually flat feet due to thousands of years of subterranean dwelling. They fall easily."

I've never heard of that. "So why not have the sign in Martian, since it's just for them? Why translate it to Standard?"

The man is clearly aghast at the idea. "And look like sectarian rubes? Not in the Chance Fleet. We offer a species-inclusive experience."

"Uh…right." I really have no response for that. It seems I have much to learn about interstellar travel and the intricacies of interspecies relations.

"You're in cabin 25J. Right this way, please." Without waiting to make sure I'm following, the guy begins a journey of ponderous twists and turns that finally ends with him planting himself parallel to a door and gesturing to it as if it were the grand prize on some lightstream gameshow. He fits a small fob into the lock mechanism and does the *look at what you could win* gesture again, so I scuttle sideways into the room like a frightened crab.

I set my carry-on atop the only piece of furniture in the room: a small ledge that will fold down from the wall to form a table. Or a desk. Or is it a seat? One thing's for sure: I'm not going to have to worry about getting up to retrieve something from the other side of the room. If I stretched my arms out, I could brush both sides of the room with my fingertips. The space is only slightly longer on the other axis.

"So...where's the bed?" I don't want be taken for one of those sectarian rubes he'd spoken so scathingly of, even if I am one. But the brochure on the travel channel of the lightstream had mentioned beds, and in a few hours, I'll need to sleep. I intend to keep to a strict schedule of sleeping and waking. Fatigue is a leading cause of fatal mishaps.

"Very easy to operate!" The man springs into action. He gently places my bag on the floor, then pulls what I'd taken for a piece of abstract art on the wall and folds it down, combining it with the table/desk/whatever to form a bed. It's kind of amazing.

"And if you need a chair, you do this." He shows me how to push the bed back into the wall and pull out other structures, which fold together to make a chair.

Quite clever, really. The designers had packed a lot of function into a tiny space.

"Your storage compartment is here." He touches a panel in the wall that pops out to reveal a one-meter by one-meter storage shelf. "And, of course, your lightstream is here." He gestures to the opposite wall, the one that would be oriented near the foot of the bed, if it were assembled. The widescreen seems oversized for the tiny space.

The man holds out a flat rectangle. "This is your control for it."

I accept the shiny black thing. It's much fancier than the one I'd had at home. I gave my lightstream to Mrs. Redding down the hall a week ago. Better to buy a new one when I get to Mebdar IV. Shipping it would cost just as much and it would probably get broken in the process anyway.

"There's a virtual tour of the ship on the home channel, so you'll be able find your way to any part of the ship. Room service is available, and the dining room never closes. Is there anything else I can help you with?"

"No, I think that covers it. Thank you."

"Excellent, Mr. Kenny. My name is Gus. If there's anything you should need, don't hesitate to let me know."

He places the key fob in my palm and as he turns to go, my bladder reminds me of something I've forgotten. "Oh, excuse me, Gus. Where is the—" And I get stuck. How to refer to the toilet without my rube-ishness showing? "I mean, where do I—"

Gus understands and saves me from my unworldliness. "The water closet is out your door and to the right, two sections down. The shower room is to the left, three sections down."

Separate toilets and showers. Apparently, my morning routine will need a little bit of an adjustment.

"Thank you, Gus."

He gives me a jaunty *I like the way those pants fit you* kind of wave and leaves. Apparently, that gesture means something else here. I try to commit that fact to memory, so I won't misinterpret the intentions of my fellow passengers.

I pick up my bag from the floor and place it in the storage compartment, then sit on the chair. Alone. In an otherwise empty, blandly cream-colored room. Others might find this disconcertingly boring.

I find it pleasantly safe.

Since I'll be on board for three weeks, I need to know the layout—particularly the emergency evacuation routes, as well as any locations that have particularly incendiary or explodey bits. I turn on the lightstream for the virtual tour of the *Second Chance*.

Onscreen, a pretty Garbdorian shows the way through the ship, stopping in all the notable locations to explain the amenities and services available. She looks vaguely familiar but I can't figure out where I might have seen her.

"A benefit of being a guest of the Chance Fleet is that we include boarding privileges at all of our ports along the way. Depending on your route and destination, you might have the opportunity to enjoy sightseeing at a variety of planets and space stations."

I pause the stream. She freezes in place, smiling at me. I study her, from her pale green hair that hangs in a chin-length bob, all the way down to her surprisingly sensible shoes. She could almost pass for a human, except that her golden-tan skin has a gentle luminescence, which quite literally gives her a glow. But who is she?

I'm certain I've never met her in person. And though she's pretty, she doesn't have the jaw-dropping looks of a movie star, so I don't think she's an actress.

After staring at her face for a few minutes, I give up and let the tour conclude with a look at the pub conveniently located adjacent to the dining room. Like I need some drunken idiot spilling his beverage on the floor and creating a slip-and-fall hazard. No thank you.

The Chance Fleet logo flashes on the screen, accompanied by a jingle about comfort and quality. So far, so good. I only hope this ship continues to live up to that promise.

My bladder tells me that I can no longer put off venturing out of my cabin. With a deep breath, I open the door to whatever mayhem might occur on a starship.

I PEEK into the corridor before stepping out. It's empty. I hope to attend to my needs and get back to my cabin before boarding is complete. Once the *Second Chance* is full, I'll be crossing paths with all manner of people.

Along the way, I notice a sign that says, *Beware of invisibility*. I try to figure out what that could mean. None of the currently-known species are capable of invisibility. Thank goodness. I have a complex about invisible forces. But by this point, I'm sure that's no surprise to you.

The water closet is just where Gus had described, and I'm pleased to find no one inside. I walk into a stall, then realize with a sinking sensation that it hadn't occurred to me to research precisely how to pee in space. The facilities do not remotely resemble those on Earth. In front of me I have an alarming amount of hose attached to a sort of seat that juts out of the wall.

I face the contraption. The alignment seems iffy, so I turn around. That seems like a way worse idea.

As I turn to once more face the disturbing apparatus, my eye catches on a diagram located at forehead level on the side wall of the stall.

I proceed to study a series of stick-figure representations that I know, right then and there, will forever change how I look at the universe. I can't tell if they're depicting what to do or what not to do. The illustrations grow increasingly disturbing, and each one only mystifies me further. One in particular leaves me feeling vaguely victimized.

Clearly, this facility had been created with numerous species in mind, and its engineers had attempted to create an evacuation system that could not only accommodate these differing physiologies, but could also perform in a potentially zero-G environment.

The diagrams are situated from left to right and bottom to top, so that by the time I discard several of the increasingly perplexing images as flat-out anatomically impossible, I have to hop to see them. Given that my bladder is near to bursting already, this creates a supremely dicey situation.

Finally, desperation gets the best of me. I yank the end of the hose from the wall, lean in, and let go, praying that I'm not peeing into some other species' sink or something.

My relief afterward is so great that I sag against the wall.

When I imagined the dangers of interstellar travel, I hadn't even considered the risk of difficulty with such basic needs. What else had I failed to anticipate?

I WALK AWAY from the water closet feeling the same as I had when I was eight and a classmate had explained to me where babies came from: confused and embarrassed and wishing I could return to my previous state of innocence.

I had intended to return to my cabin to order some room service, but if I keep walking, I'll end up in the pub. And the pub now seems like where I need to be. My nerves are on edge and a carefully measured dose of alcohol will smooth them out just a little, and leave my reflexes no worse off. It's early enough that the pub shouldn't be too busy, or have customers who are already getting sloppy.

On Earth, if you go to the bar, you sit on a stool and a well-groomed bartender will say, "What are you having?"

On the *Second Chance*, the bartender is a seven-foot-tall Mebdarian with pink skin. A mutant, apparently. Systems with a lot of natural radiation tend to have a higher incidence of children who develop mutations. Instead of asking me what I'm having, she points at me and says, "Backdoor Special."

Oh god, does she know what had happened in the water closet?

But then she faces the other direction and reaches for a bottle. Some sort of furious activity ensues, almost like a vicious struggle but with only one person. Then she turns around and slaps a glass down in front of me. She watches me expectantly.

It's a big glass. About twice the diameter of a regular drinking glass, and just as tall. Inside, a neon orange drink fizzes. No straw, no ice, no little umbrella. Just a big-ass drink and a giant pink woman waiting for me to try it.

Using both hands, I tip the glass toward me and take a sip. Bright citrus flavor bursts on my tongue, acidly tart yet sweet, with a fruity sort of alcohol flavor.

"Delicious," I say.

The bartender nods in satisfaction. "I have a knack for picking drinks for people. So I do."

Who's going to argue with a seven-foot mutant?

A new voice comes from behind me. "Best drinks I've ever had on a starship. I take the *Second Chance* just for the pub."

I probably look stupid staring at the newcomer, but it's the girl from the lightstream tour, live and in person. Her skin has that same luminescence in person, and it's kind of dazzling.

She gives me a little smile that tells me she probably gets this reaction a lot. "Plus, the fact that I fly free for being a brand ambassador. But I'd pay if I had to."

She sets her empty glass on the bar and pushes it toward the bartender. "Another one?"

The pink woman reaches for a bottle and another struggle ensues as she prepares the drink. It's hard not to stare in fascination.

But I also want to stare at the green-haired woman. She still seems familiar somehow.

She accepts her freshly-made drink, which is spiked with an extra-long purple straw, and she takes a long taste.

"What is it?" I ask. The color of the beverage is ghastly. A gray-green pus sort of color.

"A Thunderstorm. Smoke-infused Garbdorian gin with a hint of lime."

I don't care for the sound of that. I'll stick with my Backdoor Special, however unfortunate its name.

I want to ask her questions, but fear coming across as a rube.

She smiles and extends her hand. "Greta Saltz. I take it you've seen the tour on the lightstream?"

"Charlie Kenny." I intend to say more, but the bartender leans toward us and it's awkward not to include her in the introductions. "And you are?"

"Call me Pinky."

I really don't want to. If I call her that, and then she calls me something based on the way I look, it could become a whole thing. I do not want to have a thing with someone who is seven feet tall.

Greta seems to understand my concerns. "Pinky's the best," she assures me.

"Well it's nice to meet you, Pinky, and you too, Greta." I look around the pub. "It's nice and quiet in here."

"It'll be busy once we leave the space dock, and then stay busy until we get to the next one." Greta leans back against the stool next to me. I'd never get away with a precarious lean like that. It would be so easy for the stool top to shift and dump me right on the floor. At best, I'd bust my ass, but more likely, I'd break my neck. I envy her devil-may-care attitude toward secure footing and balance.

I turn back to my drink, only to find Pinky has leaned way into my space and her face is only inches from mine. I pull back and almost fall off my stool.

"You're a jumpy one, aren't you?" Pinky asks, not withdrawing one bit.

"Ah..." I stammer like an idiot. I'm not making a good impression on Greta, I'm certain. But I'd rather take the blame for being jumpy than accuse Pinky of not understanding the personal space requirements of an Earther. "I guess so. It's my first time in space."

Greta smiles and I know she understands my predicament.

Pinky nods. "Everyone has a first time. You stick with Pinky. I'll look after you."

I'm not sure whether to be alarmed or comforted, but Greta tips her glass at me. "Lucky you. Pinky likes you. She picks her friends carefully."

"Well, then I'm honored." I offer my hand to my new pink friend.

She stares at it like I've offered her a dead mouse. "Put that away and drink your Backdoor."

I do as I'm told.

Rather than edging away with an increasing air of revulsion, Greta gives me some amused side-eye.

I take a gulp of my drink and decide to push my luck. "When I was watching that virtual tour, I felt like you were familiar, but I couldn't figure out why."

"I'm a brand ambassador for a number of companies. You've probably seen me doing infovids or something."

"Oh. That makes sense. So that's what you do for a living?"

She makes an airy gesture with the hand holding her drink. "More or less. I travel around a lot, doing contract work like that."

"That sounds exciting."

Her smile turns wry. "Sometimes. Other times it's tedious. But we all have to make a living. What do you do?"

"I'm a statistician."

"Really?" Instead of looking bored or suddenly uninterested, she appears intrigued. "What do you calculate?"

"I do regression analytics to determine past behavior, in order to predict future behavior."

"Like for advertising?"

"Sometimes. Other times it's to analyze general behavior patterns for other marketing purposes, or for improving public services."

"Wow. It must be really interesting to find patterns in what people do."

"I've always thought so," I agree. "Though it seems dull to most people."

"I think it's great." She stops leaning and sits on the stool facing me. "Much more interesting than showing a camera around a ship or telling a large assembly about a new variety of banking options." She takes several gulps of her Thunderstorm.

I want to ask her why she does it if she doesn't like it, but that's too personal. A lot of people work the job that's available to them, rather than the one they'd prefer to do. Instead, I make a vaguely agreeable sound and work at emptying my giant glass at least halfway. I worry that if I don't drink most of it, I'll insult Pinky. And I don't want to find out what Pinky does to people who insult her.

A silence falls between Greta and me as we sip our drinks. Not the uncomfortable oh-shit-what-do-I-say-now kind. Just kind of a mutual contemplation. Somehow, this makes me like Greta far more than idle chitchat would have.

Pinky claps a plate on the bar in front of me, and another in front of Greta. "You two should eat before the crowd comes in and it gets too loud to hear. I ordered you both a Pinky Surprise. On the house."

"That's very generous of you," I say, though I'm a little afraid of what the surprise might be. "Thank you."

Greta murmurs her thanks as well. Her response leads me to believe that Pinky regularly keeps her fed.

Saying that the sandwich could have fed me for two days is no overstatement. It's fully eight inches tall, and alongside a pile of what appears to be some sort of breaded and fried vegetable.

I peek at Greta to see how she handles the mammoth. She casts me a sidelong glance and winks. With her palm, she smashes the thing down, reducing its height by a good two inches. Then she picks up a steak knife and cuts it into nine segments.

I follow suit and find that a mere one-ninth of the sandwich is fairly manageable, though I have to gnaw at it like a rat rather than take what I'd consider to be normal bites. But whatever. When in space, do as the space-farers do.

My first bite comes as a surprise. The sandwich is delicious. Some sort of salty synthetic meat layered up with fresh vegetables on a brown bread. It's all brought together by a creamy sauce that reminds me vaguely of mayonnaise and dill, combined with licking a battery that has both charges on one end. Zingy.

Two sections of Pinky Surprise and a few of the fried things later, I'm stuffed. I get through half my drink and am trying to figure out how to break it to Pinky that I can't finish it all when Greta says, "I think I'm going to avoid the crowd and duck back into my cabin. Mind if I get this to go?"

Relieved, I say, "That sounds like a good idea."

Pinky sweeps up both plates and my drink. "You bet." She retreats to the back side of her workspace.

"She seems really great," I say to Greta. How I've lucked into meeting two genuinely nice people, I have no idea. But every normal distribution has outliers, statistically speaking.

"She's the best." Greta smiles and slips off her stool just as Pinky returns. She takes the square takeout box that Pinky slides across the bar to her. "Well, goodnight, you two. I'm sure I'll see you again soon."

I pick up my own takeout container and the to-go cup that still holds a whole lot of Backdoor. "I hope so. It was great meeting both of you. I was worried about this voyage, but so far so good."

They both smile, and I walk back to my cabin feeling encouraged. It's a strange sensation, but pleasant. I hope I'm not setting myself up for disaster by letting myself enjoy it.

Loud knocking wakes me. I slept well and it isn't too hard to rouse myself. When I'd returned to my cabin the night before, I'd been surprised to find that my room had been reconfigured for nighttime, with the bed folded out and fresh linens impeccably smoothed over it. The brochures hadn't mentioned this attention to detail, but I like the feeling of being looked after.

On bare feet, I take three small steps to the door and push the button for the callbox. "Yes?"

"It's Gus, Mr. Kenny. I'm sorry to bother you, but you didn't register your desired time for reveille service."

"Oh." I slide the door open. "I'm sorry. There are a few things I haven't quite gotten the hang of about this kind of travel."

Gus stands at the door, bright-eyed and impeccably dressed in his fancy steward's uniform. He hands me a bag and I realize it holds my clothes, which I'd sent out the night before for laundering. "Do you prefer a later waking call, or would you rather have no waking call at all?"

"Uh, I can probably do without it. Thank you."

"Of course, Sir. Do you wish to return to bed, or shall I continue with your reveille service?"

I don't want to make him come back later. I'm sure he has a lot of better things to do. "Now is fine."

"Very good."

I squeeze myself into the corner and he enters my cabin, where he proceeds to efficiently reconfigure the bed into a table and chair and wipe the surface of the lightstream. After this burst of activity, he steps back, apparently waiting for something. Am I supposed to tip him? It's an archaic custom, but maybe I should. On the other hand, if I do and it's the wrong thing to do, it might mark me as a rube. I already know how he feels about rubes.

I hedge by asking a question. "Gus, I noticed a sign down the hall, near the water closet. It said *Beware of invisibility*. What does that mean?"

"That's just a reminder to open doors slowly. Some species startle easily."

"I guess that makes sense."

Silence falls between us again. "Is there anything else I can do for you, sir?" Gus prompts.

"Oh! No, everything's great. Thank you, Gus."

"Pleased to oblige. Let us know if there's anything we can help you with. Breakfast is underway in the dining room, if you're hungry."

Surprisingly, I am. "I could use something to eat. Thank you."

Speaking of food, I managed to put the rest of Pinky's sandwich and drink into the pulper last night. Fortunately, there's one at the corridor junction just past my cabin. The recycling vac is right next to it, so I was able to dispose of the containers too. I feel a little bad about throwing the food away, but there's no way to keep it fresh in my cabin, and it's better for Pinky to think I enjoyed all of it. She's been so nice and I don't want to hurt her feelings.

Thanks to a little research via the lightstream, I approach the water closet with more confidence this time around. Turns out I'd gotten it mostly right on my first attempt. I'd only failed to set the evacuation unit to a sanitation cycle to prepare it for the next user. Which means I'd been one of *those* jerks, but it won't happen again.

Still in my pajamas and carrying the bag with my clothes down the corridor, I proceed to do what I consider to be a phenomenal job of taking a shower like a pro.

It helps that it isn't much different from a shower on Earth, and that I was smart enough to research it before giving it a whirl.

I dress and put my pajamas in the laundry bag, then send them for cleaning. The attendant tells me they'll arrive with my evening bed service (which sounds like something more exciting than it is, but it's still kind of nice in its own way).

Right. Breakfast then.

My recent small successes and pleasant surprises all sink down to my toes as I enter the dining room.

So. Many. Forks.

A weight on my chest forces the air out of my lungs and I find myself struggling to breathe.

No. No. I can't.

I feel for the wall and put my back to it. Using it for support, I slide my way back through the doorway and into the corridor. As the clank of silverware against dishes recedes, air gradually fills my lungs.

I close my eyes, trying to get a grip. Dr. Ramalama versed me well in many techniques for managing panic attacks. I begin mentally plotting a normal distribution. Within minutes, my terror recedes and my heartbeat slows to normal. I can't go back into that dining room, though. Yet, I'm hungry.

A Pinky sandwich is what I need. Nobody uses forks in a pub. But it won't be open this early.

A steward approaches with a look of concern. "Sir, can I be of assistance? Are you lost?"

"No. I was just..." being an anxiety-ridden redshirt. But I can't say that. "When does the pub open?"

"It never closes."

"It doesn't?"

The steward nods, looking pleased. "Given that we sometimes have nocturnal passengers, we pride ourselves on providing round-the-clock services."

"That wasn't in the brochures."

That takes the pleased look off my host's face. Oops. I didn't mean it to sound like a complaint. Damn my lack of finesse.

"Not to argue, sir, but the third click-through of the brochure, second paragraph up, reads, 'Unlimited time limit is permitted for drinking.'"

Uhm. Right. How stupid of me to have overlooked that very obvious wording for "all-day bar."

"I must have missed that part. I'm sorry to trouble you."

The steward regains the look of pride that seems better suited for a war hero or something, but apparently, the attendants of the *Second Chance* take their jobs very seriously. "It's never any trouble at all. We're always glad to help. Do you need assistance getting to the pub?"

"No, thank you, I know the way."

"Very good sir." With a tiny bow, my host departs.

After that exchange, I alter my breakfast plans to include a drink.

As soon as I step into the bar, I see Pinky. She's hard to miss.

"Didn't expect to see you here," I say. "I thought you'd be up late last night."

"I was. I don't need much sleep."

"What's that like?" I ask.

Pinky stops wiping the bar and gives me her full attention. "Mostly fine. Boring sometimes. I like being around people, and that's tough when most of them spend a third of their time sleeping."

"Makes sense. How much do you sleep?"

"About an hour a day." She studies me. "You hungry?"

I consider my response carefully in relation to her idea of portion sizes. "Just a little. I could use a small snack."

Pinky nods knowingly. "I'm not that into breakfast, either. I know just the thing." She retreats to the drink-prep area where she also orders food for her guests.

She returns a few moments later with a tall, skinny glass full of a clear beverage. After the previous night's colors, I'm a little disappointed. But when she sets it in front of me, she drops in a clear, round ice cube and the drink immediately turns a deep blue.

"Morning Wakeup." Her eyes are fixed on the glass.

It occurs to me that she isn't going to move until I taste it. "Mm. Like tart blueberries, but crisp and refreshing."

She seems satisfied by that. "It has more kick than you'd think. I've flattened more than one rude asshole with a couple of 'on the house' Morning Wakeups. That's why I gave you a small glass."

Pinky's free food and drinks do not always come from a place of generosity, then. That somehow makes her more interesting to me and I wonder what her life is like. "It's delicious. Thanks."

She seems to ignore that, but I know she heard it because she no longer stands there frozen. She wheels away to mix some drinks, which are promptly whisked away on a tray by a porter. Room service, I suppose. Or maybe people in the dining room. I imagine them all getting drunk and going into a stabby fork frenzy.

A shiver goes down my spine and I take a gulp of my Wakeup.

A porter with a tray arrives and, rather than accept it, Pinky points her chin toward me.

"Here you are, sir." The porter sets the tray in front of me.

I'm relieved to see a normal-sized sandwich and a small pile of tater tots. Just like that, I start to fall for Pinky. Not in a romantic way, but in a deeper she-gets-me kind of way. Four years of therapy with Dr. Ramalama, and she never came close to really getting me, but in less than one day, Pinky has my full confidence. I'll have to give that some serious thought.

I don't know what's in the sandwich, but it's peppery, chewy, and delicious. "Are tater tots common in the Mebdar system?" I ask. I always thought they were an Earth thing.

Pinky looks at me like I'm a silly child. "Mebdarians invented tater tots."

I'm not sure that's true, but I nod agreeably. "I've always loved them."

Pinky nods back, like we're part of some secret club. "Fried potato and salt. What's not to love?" She holds up her hand in a *stop* gesture and I stare at her stupidly until I realize what she wants. I toss her a tot. She catches it easily and pops it into her mouth. "That's what I'm talkin' 'bout."

I've never had this. Never sat at a pub, never threw food at people. Never felt like a truly normal person. I've always kept myself carefully one degree away from everything around me, for the sake of self-preservation. I have a sudden and liberating feeling of freedom. I never want to leave this pub.

The tater tot that chooses that particular moment to lodge itself into my throat and begin trying to murder me should not come as a surprise. My air supply cuts off and I try to alert Pinky but I only manage to make a quiet, pathetic honk.

She's on it, though. Maybe it's a hallucination due to panic and oxygen deprivation, but all seven feet of glorious Pinky vault over the bar and she grabs me like I'm a kitten. One quick squeeze that feels like I've been stepped on by an elephant and that tot flies across the pub and hits the bulkhead.

Pinky lowers me to the ground and sits next to me, gently patting my back as I cough and gasp and my eyes water and my nose runs.

Which of course is when I notice Ms. Greta Saltz watching in horror.

"Fuck! That tater tot tried to kill Kenny!" Her eyes are wide with shock and, strangely, admiration. Garbdorians must emote admiration differently than humans do.

I cough one last time. "Charlie," I correct her. "My last name's Kenny."

"Right. Sorry." Greta looks chagrined. "I tend to forget which planets do the family-name-first thing."

"That's okay," I say, wiping my face and pretending that she hasn't just witnessed my near-death at the potatoey hands of a tiny fried blob, even as Pinky gently sits me back on my stool.

Greta's a champ though, because she pretends right along with me. She asks Pinky for a lushfruit muffin and a glass of yak milk, straight up.

"Just one," Pinky says to her warningly. "You know how you get."

I really want to know how she gets, but am not brave enough to ask.

I eyeball my tater tots. Not eating them would be uncool, as it would ruin my pretending-my-horrible-almost-death-never-happened mystique, which I feel is working for me. But while I'd enjoyed them before, I'm now engaged in a death match against them. In this corner, a pile of starchy little murderers, and in the other corner, Charlie Kenny, master of the unlikely. Well, not the master. If I were the master, I wouldn't have to worry about this kind of crap.

Whatever. I tear a tot in two, dunk it in the orange sauce, and carefully chew. Hah. Take that, tater.

The night before, Greta had been casually friendly. Now, however, she seems...well, interested. Which is the opposite of how my encounters with women usually go, and understandably makes me question everything in my life up to this point.

She turns chatty. As she tears the top off her muffin then pulls off little bits to poke into her mouth, she asks me questions about life on Earth, my work, my background, and so forth. Being a polite conversationalist, I ask similar things of her, and learn quite a lot about her. Which I don't mind at all.

"What about school?" she asks, veering away from questions

about my family, which inevitably result in ghastly answers. I'm not sure if she turns from the topic of my family for my sake or hers, but the change of pace is refreshing. Sort of.

"Oh, you know," I say airily. "Explosions in chemistry class, taking the elevator instead of the stairs, and always making sure I sit near an exit."

"Why?" she asks, fascinated.

"Well, it's a risk," I admit. "If a rabid boar comes barreling into the room, I'm right there within chomping distance. But it's more likely that something will happen inside the room. An earthquake, for example. And access to the exit becomes a critical thing."

"So there was never a rabid boar." She smiles, seeming charmed by the idea.

"No, there was. But it got electrocuted by a loose wire in the doorway so it worked out."

The smile freezes on her face. "Damn."

"Yeah. Two negatives made a positive." As soon as I say it, I mentally kick myself. Math jokes are not the way to impress girls.

But she laughs. "I guess it did."

"What about you?" I ask. "What was school like?"

But she made a dismissive gesture. "Nothing interesting. The same old stuff. Valedictorian. Prom queen. Blah blah blah."

"What about university?" I ask.

"I only went for a year, then it closed down due to a goat infestation."

Now that sounds like my kind of luck. Maybe we have something in common after all. "How does a university get a goat infestation?"

Her eyes widen and she shakes her head. "It was the strangest thing. One day we were in class and the next, goats had taken over the school. I don't know if you're familiar with goats, but once they've decided to be somewhere, it's really hard to convince them otherwise."

I, in fact, have no familiarity with goats. I have no regrets about that. "So then what?"

"I went to a jai-alai tournament the next day, and someone was taking video. An executive at Spark Cola saw it and noticed me in the crowd. A couple of messages and one meeting later, I was their new brand ambassador."

That sounds exceedingly against the odds to me. "How many people were at the tournament?"

"Ten thousand or so."

Jai-alai must be way more popular where she's from than it is on Earth. But I have trouble even beginning to compute the odds of someone picking her out of a crowd of ten thousand and tracking her down to give her a job. A job that thousands of people would have eagerly auditioned for. But no. Greta Saltz got the job without even trying.

Apparently, she's just one of those people that fortune smiles upon. The opposite of me. That first job with Spark Cola had started Greta on her life of travel and adventure.

It sounds positively fascinating to me, but she seems bored by it all. "What about your work? Any natural disasters or hostage situations?"

Her avid interest in my foibles makes me wonder if she's ridiculing me. But Pinky looks on curiously, and I don't think she'd allow someone to be that kind of mean in her pub.

As we talk, Greta tears the bottom portion of her muffin into pieces and spreads them across her plate. Her process of eating fascinates me. Does she always obliterate her food this way? She cut that sandwich last night into pieces, but I'd thought at the time that was merely a matter of handling the size issue. Perhaps not.

"What's your destination, Charlie?" she asks. "I'm headed for Mebdar III."

I'm not sorry to move the conversation away from the disasters in my life. "I'm going to the end of the line—Mebdar IV."

Greta's brow furrows. "The retirement planet? Did you take a job there or something?"

Man, I really wish I could say yes to that. "No, I can work remotely from pretty much anywhere."

"Oh, you're visiting someone?"

I suppress a sigh. "No. I'm moving there."

Yep, there it is. The look I'm used to getting from people who see me holding onto a staircase railing for dear life, or refusing to cross a busy road.

"Why?"

Time to give her the big truth, which will surely have her recoiling like a frightened turtle. Though perhaps she already suspects, given our conversation. "I'm a—" my voice catches. Probably a residual piece of tater tot. I clear my throat. "I'm a redshirt."

I don't think I've ever said the words out loud before, except during therapy. People like me don't advertise our genetic heritage. Not surprisingly, it scares the shit out of people to be near someone who has a one-hundred percent chance of dying in a terrible and unlikely way—and perhaps taking some innocent bystanders with him.

But when I chance a look at Greta, she seems fascinated. A peek at Pinky reveals a total lack of concern. If anything, she looks bored. But then, what does she have to worry about? The woman could probably eat the *Second Chance* if she wanted to, and complain that it didn't have enough salt.

"Wow," Greta says. "I've never met one before."

I have no answer for that. She said it like being a redshirt was interesting somehow, not a death sentence. Sudden doubt about her intelligence makes me squint at her.

"I mean, I'm sure it sucks," she says quickly.

"You could say that. My nana's a cyborg."

She clicks her tongue in commiseration. "Ah, and cyborg cookies are total rubbish, aren't they?"

"Yeah."

Silence falls over us. We had both stopped eating and I feel uncomfortable. Exposed. I wish I'd never said anything about my history. I could have been anyone before all this, as far as they knew. Now I'm just...a redshirt.

I stand. "If you'll excuse me, I have some work to do in my cabin." It isn't a lie, but Greta and Pinky surely know I just want to get out of there. They play along, though, and I thank Pinky again for the breakfast and for the life-saving.

She shrugs both off. "Come back for lunch. I'll make sure you get something really good that won't kill you."

I have no intention of that. I know they'll see a redshirt every time they look at me from now on. "I'll have to see if I get done in time," I hedge.

Pinky gives me a sad look and nods. I don't even look at Greta as I make my getaway.

Back in my cabin, I heave a sigh. It had been nice, pretending to be a normal person. For a minute there, I was even happy. I thought maybe my luck would hold for a little longer, that maybe I could get a glimpse of a normal life.

I sit and turn on the lightstream. It will have to be my companion for the rest of this trip. I'll start on the statistics work tomorrow.

It's almost worse, really, to have had such a good start to this trip. It raised my hopes, making the fall back to my reality hard to take.

AFTER FALLING asleep to an old robot western on the lightstream, I wake up to a banging sound. Falling to the floor in a tangle of sheets, sure that doom has arrived, is not the best way to start a day. But I've begun enough days that way to be able to pick myself up with relative equanimity.

"Open up, Charlie, we've arrived at Posytin!" Greta's unmistakable voice reaches me before I even make it to the door.

My shoulders sag. Why has Greta sought me out? Does she want to make sure I didn't choke to death on my own saliva while I slept?

When the door opens, she stands there, looking excited and pretty. The sight of her happiness has me swallowing my words—which amount to a polite way of saying, *Buzz off*.

She wedges her bright personality right into my doorway, preventing me from closing the door or telling her I want to be alone. "Come on, grab whatever you need and let's go! You're going to love Posytin. We have three hours of stopover before we get underway again."

My mouth is too full of my suddenly gigantic tongue to get any words out. I suspect a rift in the space-time continuum. Or entry into a parallel dimension. Sure, the odds of those are infinitesimal, but either possibility seems more likely than Greta Saltz wanting to go day tripping with a guy who'd nearly gotten killed by a piece of potato the day before. I run the numbers in my head and decide it must be a parallel dimension.

"You're still in your jammies?" She looks at me with incredulity. "Come on, there are things to see!" She takes a step closer to me and grasps the hem of my shirt as if to shuck it up over my head.

I find the ability to speak. Sort of. "Blaahg!" I say.

I'd like to tell you that this is a Garbdorian word for *please remove your hands from my clothing*, but I'd be lying. At least I'd managed to become verbal. I back away from her. Not far, given the lack of space in my cabin, but her arms fall to her sides.

"Should I give you a minute?" she asks.

"Uh, yeah. Is there a package from the laundry out there?"

She goes back into the corridor and checks the delivery bin. "Yes." She returns holding a clothing bag.

I take it from her awkwardly. "Right. I guess I'll get dressed then."

We stare at each other for about three and a half seconds, then she takes a step backward, into the corridor. "I'll be waiting right here." She points to the deck plate below her feet.

I close the door in her pretty golden face. Which is rude, and I'm immediately sorry for it, but I'm so thrown for a loop that I barely know my ass from an exhaust pipe.

I put on my clothes and stuff my pajamas into the clothing bag to send it out for laundering. Taking a deep breath, I open the door.

"What do you want with me?" I ask. Again, rude. I know. Like I said—ass versus exhaust pipe.

Rather than being put off by my lack of manners, she smiles. "It's your first trip away from Earth, right?"

"Yes."

"That means this is your first trip to Posytin. I want to show it to you."

"I don't think you do. I mean, I'm not..." Not safe. Not normal. Not the kind of guy you want to hang around with. "...like other people," I finish lamely.

"Neither am I," she answers. "Let's go."

3
———

IT ALL HAPPENS IN A BLUR, and before I know it, I'm about to disembark from the *Second Chance* to go sightseeing. I recalculate the odds of having slipped into a parallel universe.

Leaving the ship means going down an elevator that I hadn't seen when arriving on the ship. Above it, a sign reads, *Do not use elevator. Please use elevator.*

"I think this one's broken," I say. "Is there another?"

Greta laughs. "Never mind the sign. It means *do* use the elevator."

"But it says not to use it."

The thing opens. It might actually look like the gate to hell, or, more likely, one of my complexes has come roaring to life. But Greta takes my hand and pulls me in. I'm so stunned by her touch that I'm like a deer in headlights. I suspect I'd walk right into a lion's mouth if she led me there by the hand.

What is wrong with me?

As we stand there and the doors close, though, I get a very bad feeling in my stomach. Something like a porcupine that's been lit on fire. But we begin to descend and Greta turns her head slightly to smile at me. When we get to the bottom and the doors reopen, I remember to breathe. That could have been really awful—elevators are not kind to my people. But somehow with Greta, it had been okay. So far.

The Posytin space port turns out to be small and calm. Provincial, even. Fresh-faced teenagers carry baskets full of paper brochures, which they offer to people as we filter through the airlocks. A freckle-faced boy holds one out to me, and he looks so earnest that I hurriedly accept it.

"We won't need that. I know all the best places to visit." Greta leads me through the small station and out to Posytin itself. Or whatever town within Posytin this is. I know nothing of the naming habits of such places.

She pauses on the sidewalk, taking in a deep breath. "Doesn't it smell wonderful here?"

I take a tiny, cautious sniff. I have no plans of snorting a bee up my nose. Or whatever insects they have here. I must admit the aroma is nice, though. "Is that flowers?"

"Yes!" She spreads her arms in the air. "This little planet provides most of the flowers you'll find along this trade route. A good bit beyond that, too. That's pretty much their whole reason for being: growing flowers and flora tourism."

"People go traveling just to look at flowers?"

"Sure." Greta shrugs. "There are far worse reasons. I think it's nice. I love the chance to get fresh air and some time outdoors."

"Right. You spend a lot of your time traveling around on ships."

"Yeah. I like it, but it gets a little stifling sometimes. All that recirculated air." She scrunches up her nose, looking cute.

"So where are we going?"

"The best garden on Posytin."

"What makes it the best?"

"I won't spoil the surprise. But they also have a stand with fried flowers that you dip in a sweet sauce. It's amazing."

Not only am I not sure about eating in front of her again, I'm really dubious about eating flowers. But I stay quiet.

A piece of paper skitters across the ground and lands in the same spot as Greta's next step. She bends, reaches, and comes back up with a rectangular paper with curly blue writing on it.

"What's that?" I ask.

"Local money."

"Paper money?" I'm amazed. I've never seen physical currency. Banking is usually done through the First Interplanetary Bank, in entirely digital form. It's clean, efficient, and a barrier to illegal activity since it's so easily tracked. Not that illegal activity is impossible. Just risky.

"Something they do for the tourists. Getting people to exchange their money for this stuff is like letting them have play money. It's fun, like a game, and they spend it accordingly."

"How much is it?" I can't decipher the script.

"Fifty marks."

"Is that a lot?"

Greta gives me a cheeky grin. "Enough to cover our activities here. Including a souvenir for you."

"I don't need a souvenir." I'm not much of a collector of kitsch. Or of anything, really.

"Sure you do. This is your first visit to a planet that isn't Earth. That's pretty cool."

She resumes walking, which saves me from having to reply.

We arrive at a tall, wooden arch emblazoned with *Welcome to Waterfall Garden*.

I freeze like a dog that just realized he's on the way to the vet. "There's a waterfall in there?"

"Just a little one. It's nice." She tries to nudge me forward.

I resist. "Define *little*."

"Tiny." She makes a vague gesture. "Nothing to worry about."

"I don't want to drown today. Or ever."

She rolls her eyes and puts her arm around my waist. "You're not going to drown. Come on."

Her arm. Is around. My waist. I'm entirely incapable of resistance as she propels me through the arch. Once she's sure I'm coming along, her arm falls away, but still I follow her lead.

A man approaches, dozens of loops of interwoven flowers draped over his forearm. With a happy smile, he plucks one and holds it up. An offer.

Greta nods and the man gently places the flower crown on her head. "Thank you," she says warmly.

"You're welcome. If anyone asks, tell them where you got it." He winks at her.

"I will."

As we walk, she puts a hand to the flowers. "Like it?"

"It's pretty," I admit, though I've never particularly cared for flowers. But they look nice on her.

We walk along for several minutes, down a wide path with flowering hedges on each side. The roar of water in the distance gets louder as we go. We turn a corner and there it is, a seven-foot-tall waterfall, with a cascade of frothing water rushing over.

I take a step back. Sure, it's small, as waterfalls go. But fear shoots up my spine and no amount of tugging from Greta is going to get me past that point.

Her smile falls away and worry fills her eyes. "Okay. Okay. I'm sorry. Let's go this way instead."

She pulls me off the path, between a pair of trees with long purple flowers spiraling down. The noise of the water nearly disappears. Greta leads me deeper into the cool, damp space between the trees.

"Here." She sits with her legs folded and gestures at me to do the same.

I sit across from her.

She takes my hands and presses hers to mine, palm to palm, fingers toward the unseen sky above. Then she laces her fingers with mine. It isn't like holding hands, really. It's more like being in a secret clubhouse and we're the only two members. Which feels...nice. I've never belonged with others, and I imagine this is what belonging feels like.

"I'm sorry, I didn't think," she says. "Are you okay now?"

"Yes." Inside this little hideaway, I feel fine. I can smell all the floral aromas, along with the earthier smell beneath these trees.

"I'll be right back, then."

Before I can say anything, she trots out of our hideout, opposite of the direction we'd come in.

So, I sit there, alone, with my butt gradually growing damp from the soft dirt and leaves beneath. It isn't actually unpleasant, though. The air is fresh and smells good. No bugs are buzzing around. I wonder why. Aren't bugs attracted to flowers and trees and dirt and stuff? Maybe Posytin is just different than Earth.

Greta returns after only a few minutes, carrying a tray with pointy brown things on it. "The edible flowers I told you about. They're called heliopoppers." She takes one of the things, which is about the length of her longest finger, dips it into the sauce, then takes a crunching bite. "Mmm," she sighs, clearly delighted by the flavor. "Try one." She sets the tray between us.

I pick one up between my forefinger and thumb. It could be any fried food, really. It's brown. As far as I can tell, it smells okay. I dredge it in the sauce and take a cautious nibble.

I try really hard to be polite, since she so clearly likes the things. But they taste like deep-fried perfume, which doesn't work for me.

"Aw, you don't like them." Greta looks disappointed.

"Not in the least. Sorry. Ah..." I glance around. "Is there somewhere we could get a drink?"

I feel like I've guzzled my grandmother's cologne. The other grandma, not the cyborg one.

"Sure."

Ten minutes later, we're out of the flower garden and seated at an outdoor café. I sip an iced tea and delight in having the heliopopper taste out of my mouth.

"So, what's it like?" she asks, watching me with that look of fascination.

"What?" For a second, I think she means the tea, but then I realize she means my life.

She waves a hand in a gesture that encompassed all of me. "Being you. Nearly dying on a tater tot. Being afraid of a waterfall. All that."

I don't know how to answer. I mean, it sucks to be on edge all the time. But how can I make her understand that?

"It must be so interesting," she prompts.

Normally, I'd think she was making fun of me, but she seems...wistful. Kind of envious, even. "No. It's not interesting. It sucks. Why would you think that?" For the first time, I wonder if she might be a very special kind of stupid.

"Things happen to you!" she bursts out, suddenly agitated. "Things you don't expect. I mean, look at me. I walk into a room and I know I can have things if I want them. I walk into a garden and am given a free flower crown for no reason. Wherever I go, foods I like are sold. Whatever I want just falls into my hands. It's so. Damn. Boring!" She fires each word off like a missile.

"Wait, those flower crowns aren't free for everyone?"

"No! They cost ten marks. But I've never paid for one, not even once, in all the times I've come here. I even tried to insist once. He just wouldn't take my money!" She blows out a breath, looking incensed.

"You're mad that people give you things for free?" Yeah, this girl is definitely a few asteroids short of a shower.

"Yes! I'm tired of life being so predictable. I mean, when I walked into the pub yesterday and there you were choking on a tater tot, I was amazed. I bet you had no idea that would happen, and then it did! I sure had no idea I'd see that. Stuff like that doesn't happen around me."

"You're saying you're preternaturally lucky or something?" I crinkle my forehead, staring at her.

"Yes! It's a curse."

I fall silent, staring at her.

She sighs and sinks down into her chair. She looks lumpy and disgruntled. "I know it sounds stupid. But imagine your life as a plain white tunnel and all you do is walk down it, forever and ever and *ever*. Nothing changes. It's perfectly pleasant, but nothing ever happens. There's no excitement. No mystery. No surprises"

It sounds good to me. "I'm trying to see your life as a bad thing. My life is a tunnel full of trapdoors and fall hazards and plague germs. I know I'll never get even halfway down it because of all the obstacles in my way."

Greta straightens slowly. "I'd trade you. I'd swap a shortened lifespan for some excitement."

"I'd be happy with your plain white tunnel."

Greta makes a pouty duck sort of face, which sounds not at all cute, but it actually is. "Has anything bad happened to you when you're with me?"

I think about it. I had a good time the night I first met her. The next morning, she'd arrived just as Pinky saved my life. So, actually, not dying was a good thing that happened to me. And nothing actually bad happened at the garden. I'm surprised to answer, "No."

"And since I met you, I've had surprises. I don't know what to expect with you."

I don't know how to respond to that, so I make the manly choice of changing the subject. "We should get back to the *Second Chance*."

She looks disappointed, but seems to reconsider, then beams at me. "Okay."

We almost make it back to the spaceport when she freezes in mid-step. "Oh! Your souvenir."

"I don't need one."

"I insist." She pivots and darts toward a vendor stand that—surprise, surprise—just happens to be several feet away.

Reluctantly, I join her, grimacing at the silly *I'm a Posy Boy* t-shirts and hats. If she tries to make me accept something like that, she'll be in for another surprise today.

But she whispers something to the vendor, and he saunters to the back of the stand and bends to reach into a box beneath a table. He drops the item onto her palm and her fingers close around it before I see more than a flash of green. She reaches toward her pocket and the smiling man waves her off. She gives her thanks and we're on our way again.

It isn't until we're just about to pass through the docking gate to board the *Second Chance* that she digs into her pocket and holds her fist out to me.

I open my hand and she drops a shiny green stone onto it. It's warm from her body heat and just the right size to curl my fingers around.

"What is it?"

"It's a luck stone. You keep it with you, and rub it when you feel worried. Then it gives you luck. And since I carried it for a few minutes, I figure it should have extra luck now."

It's the sweetest gift anyone had ever given me. "Thank you. I wish I had a bad luck stone to give you." Which sounds stupid, but she knows what I mean.

She smiles sagely and as we board the ship, she says, "We'll see."

AFTER BEING OUT WITH GRETA, I feel like being daring. I know it's crazy, but I want to test my boundaries. Go wild. I bravely take a different route back to my cabin.

That may not sound like much, but for me it's huge. Taking

the same path, so I can anticipate any potential hazards, is ingrained in me. It's one of the habits my therapist had been trying to break me of for the past few years. After just two days, Greta has succeeded. Take that, Dr. Ramalama!

My eyes dart across the unknown corridor, side to side, up and down, watching for hazards. I'm being daring, not stupid. I haven't forgotten who I am and where I come from.

At the junction to the corridor leading to my cabin, I spot a red sign. It reads *Red sign means bad. Do not do the bad.*

I don't find the sign helpful. Actually, I find it terrifying. My previous sense of adventure evaporates as I look around for "the bad." What would that be?

A loud clank makes me spin around. I'd like to say it was a cool, ninja sort of spin, but in fact, I yelp like a Chihuahua that's been stepped on.

Gus stands there, holding a chaffing dish and looking at me in alarm. "Are you okay, sir?"

"Yes! Sorry. You just startled me."

"My apologies, sir. The dish slipped."

"Oh, no reason to apologize. Not your fault."

"Thank you, sir." He continues on his way.

"Gus," I call after him.

"Yes?" He pauses again.

I point to the sign. "What does that mean?"

He glances at it. "To be honest, no one knows. We should probably take it down."

"Probably a good idea," I agree.

Gus hurries out of sight and I continue on to my cabin, only mildly reassured. I will avoid the *Do not do the bad* corridor in the future. No reason to tempt fate.

I TAKE some time to decompress and process the day's events. The luck stone lays on my little fold-out table while I sit in the chair, going through some messages from work. I'll need to spend the evening creating some regression analyses, but that's fine with me. The work will be soothing after the eventful day I've had.

At the moment, though, I require food. I consider ordering in, but find myself wanting to see Pinky. I pull myself together and go to the pub.

Though it feels much later than midday to me, the pub is full of the lunch rush. Pinky spots me as soon as I come through the door, and leans against the bar, waiting for me to sit.

"You look too serious," is her greeting to me. She spins away and returns a couple minutes later with a curvy glass full of a blush-pink beverage and garnished with an orange slice.

"What is it?" I ask.

"A Happy Day."

I sip it and taste yuzu, passionfruit, and some other fruity flavors I can't identify. It's carbonated and tastes…zippy. I know that's not a flavor, but that's the only way to describe it.

"It's good."

"That particular combination of fruits has an uplifting effect," she says.

"Really? Some sort of drink alchemy to affect mood?"

She nods.

"Do you ever use your alchemy for evil, rather than good?"

A tiny smile forms on her lips, but she says nothing.

"I see." I don't know if it's the Happy Day or Pinky, but my mood lifts. "Do you know how to make a Screaming Demon?"

"Sure. But it's hard on the stomach."

I try to think of an obscure Earth drink to see if I can stump her. "How about a Flaming Butterfly?"

"Yes."

"A Bruised Mortician?" I make that one up, just to see her reaction.

"Yes, but I don't stock formaldehyde. The Ontopians are the

only ones who drink it and only one has ever come on board this ship."

I stare at her. Raising my glass, I say, "You are one heck of a woman, Pinky."

She leans forward and loudly whispers, "And they'll never find the bodies to prove it."

I pause in mid-sip, trying to figure out if she's serious or making a joke.

She watches me with a smirk. Joking, then. Probably.

"Do you believe in luck?" I didn't expect to ask that, but the question jumps out of me on its own.

She stops wiping the counter and flips the towel over her shoulder. Leaning against the bar, she appears to give the matter deep thought. "You know, I do. Some people say it's just the massiveness of the universe and the fact that unlikely things—good or bad—have to happen to someone. But I've known some people who almost never lose, and others who almost never win, and none of it has a thing to do with how they play the game. It's just their luck."

I drum my fingers on the bar, thinking about that. Pinky glances at my hand and raises an eyebrow. I stop drumming.

"Why do you think that is?" I ask.

Pinky shrugs. "Some call it karma or charisma. Or on the unlucky side, they might call it a curse or the evil eye. My people call it *kenogu*."

"What does that mean?"

"It translates roughly to 'shit happens.' More specifically, it means that you get what you get, and you can't blame reality for what it gives you. It's up to you to work with what you have."

"How do you use that in a sentence?"

She pulls the towel from her shoulder goes back to wiping the bar, which looks perfectly clean to me.

"Your *kenogu* is being a redshirt. Or, if you were to suddenly fall off your stool and break your arm, you could just say, '*Kenogu*.'

You could even use it as a verb. 'I'm going to *kenogu* my way out of here!' It's a multipurpose word."

"Those are the best kind." I can tell she agrees.

An elderly Martian approaches the bar and orders a half-dozen drinks. I fight back a laugh because that sounds like the opening line to a joke. I look back toward the table and see only one other person. I guess what they say about Martians being drinkers is true.

After the guy takes the tray of glasses to his table, Pinky begins a frenzy of beverage creation. She works four blenders simultaneously, squeezing fruit with one hand while shaking a cocktail mixer with the other, and she practically juggles swizzle sticks and garnishes. Her precision is absolute; she doesn't spill a single drop. I'm watching a master at work.

Porters come and whisk away the drinks she made. Pinky tosses her towel over her shoulder and rejoins me.

"So…do you know Greta well?" I'm hesitant to ask, but, at the moment, I only have two people I could even remotely call friends. Unless you count Gus. Which I don't. Getting paid to deliver my underwear every morning does not qualify.

Pinky plucks a straw from the bar and pokes it into the side of her mouth. The protruding part wiggles as she chews on it. "I see her frequently. We talk. I don't know if that means I know her well. I think you'd have to ask her if I know her well, since only she knows how much of herself she's revealed to me."

I hadn't thought I could be more impressed by Pinky, and here she's upped the ante again. That was damned philosophical of her.

"Okay. Does she know you well, then?"

The straw waggles wildly. "Fairly well."

"Do you trust her?"

"With what?"

Pinky's shrewdness has me examining what I really want to know. I whittle it down to one thing: "Your life."

I realize that this is the heart of the matter. By asking me to leave the ship with her, Greta had, whether she intended to or not, asked me to put my life in her hands.

And I had. Why?

Greta's cute, no doubt. Pretty. But not the exotic-vacation-sales kind of beauty that makes a person drain their life savings for a jaunt to Paradise Cove that they never even wanted.

No, it isn't mere physical attraction. Though I definitely feel something when she touches me. Not in a my-parts-are-all-tingly way, but in a way that makes me feel alive. Aware. Like things I never imagined somehow become possibilities when I'm with her.

Dare I say exciting? Excitement has always been a warning sign for me in the past. A bad thing. Red alert. Imminent death ahead.

But I feel different with her.

I realize Pinky's staring at me. "What?"

"You asked me a question, then you started staring into space. I wondered if you had a weevil in your brain."

Is that an expression or an actual thing that could happen? I'll have to look that up later. And maybe weevil repellant.

No, no weevils. I just got sidetracked by a thought. Sorry. You were saying?"

"I believe Greta has my best interests at heart," she says. "I don't expect her to be able to save my life in a battle with a bunch of bloodthirsty blagrooks, though."

"Uh, do they attack often?" I have a new thing to worry about now. Yay.

"Nah. Only once on this ship." Her face transforms into smug satisfaction and she takes the straw out of her mouth to point it at me. "I squashed 'em like bugs. Stupid blagrooks."

I fight to stay on topic and not get sidetracked by the fact that I don't know the statistical likelihood of a blagrook attack. "So, if

Greta wanted me to go sightseeing with her at the next stop, you think I'd be safe?"

Pinky wads the straw up in her large hand, tosses it into her mouth, and eats it. Is that food to her people, or is she just showing off? "Next stop is Parkorvan. Great place, but it can get dicey if you don't know your way around." She straightens with sudden purpose. "I'll go with you two. Keep you safe."

I had intended to find out more about Greta, but, somehow, I've now made a date with Pinky to play tourist on a planet that could be "dicey."

What have I done?

Two days of catching up with work for my employer and talking with Pinky at the pub go by quickly, and then I realize the catastrophic error I've committed in agreeing to our sightseeing trio.

The problem is that Parkorvan is a university planet. You might think, *Cool! Academic types, keggers, and cheap eats aplenty.* And you'd probably have a good time there.

But as I step into the brisk breeze, beneath an overcast sky, I quiver with the kind of trepidation a guinea pig would feel when skittering past a pharmacology lab.

Parkorvan isn't just an academic place. It's a premiere hub of research. Scientific research. The kind of research that tends to get out of hand, go haywire, and end up turning a planet into a dystopian nightmare. Zombies, maybe. Or a plague. Yeah, a plague sounds about right.

The air even starts to smell a little weird. I'm getting whiffs of —what is that? Eucalyptus. Is there a type of plague that's heralded by the smell of cough drops?

I shiver.

But as Pinky and Greta steer me down the main parkway, I have to admit that it's a picturesque place. Lots of people on bicycles. Everywhere I look, I see an abundance of happy-go-lucky young people. I do not find that the least bit reassuring.

I keep smelling hints of eucalyptus and my anxiety only rises higher. Trying to calm myself, I reason that if there were any reason to suspect a plague outbreak, these nice-looking young people wouldn't be going about their lives so nonchalantly. Plus, I have Greta's luck and Pinky's straight-up badassness with me. I'll be fine. Right?

I put my hand in my right pocket and rub my luck stone.

I hope no one thinks I'm playing pocket pool.

We walk for what feels like forever. I barely register the expertly manicured green areas and flower beds. I notice some students playing Frisbee and carefully align myself against Pinky so that if a damn disk comes my way, either it will turn out to be a grand prize in some contest for Greta, or Pinky will catch that shit and obliterate it.

I manage to avoid any mishaps, and, finally, Greta gestures at a huge wooden door at the front of a large stone building.

"Here we are!" She seems entirely happy and blissfully unaware of my hypervigilance.

We walk into an old library and, I have to admit, it's grand. The building has walls that rise three stories high, stacked with books upon books all the way up. I mean actual paper books. I've never seen such a thing.

"Wow." And as genuinely impressive as it is, in the back of my head, I begin calculating the odds of a book spontaneously slipping from the wall and falling three stories to land on my head.

"Isn't it beautiful?" Greta's voice is full of wonder and admiration.

I have to admit that it is.

"Pretty," is all Pinky says. Actually, she hadn't said much at all since leaving the *Second Chance*. Odd, since she has plenty to say when we're in her pub. But that's probably where she feels most at home. Maybe I'm not the only one outside my comfort zone.

Next thing I know, Greta rushes to a spiral staircase on the far side of the cavernous library and runs up it. I edge up to the bottom of the staircase and look upward at her feet, which are running in circles and carrying her ever higher. She peers over the side of the rail and beckons. "Come on!"

A sign in front of me insists that the staircase is for employees only. I scan the vicinity, waiting for some angry librarian to come mete out some punishment. But nothing. I look at Pinky. Pinky looks at me. Sighing, I grip the rail and carefully step up, slanted stair by slanted stair. Spiral staircases suck. I'm slightly reassured to know that Pinky's right behind me.

When we finally reach the top, Greta grins at us. "Come on!" she says again, darting ahead.

"Wait!" I call. "You can't just come up here. We aren't supposed to be in this part." This area has a very different feel than down below. A wide, unadorned hallway is punctuated by a series of doors on each side.

"Sure we can. It's fine. Trust me."

I want to. I've witnessed her luck before, and I really want to trust her. I just can't. I have too much history. Too much litany of the many Kennys who have died doing the most innocuous things.

But then, a voice inside me argues, *if even the most mundane thing can result in doom, why keep worrying about it? Maybe when a redshirt's time is up, it's just up, no matter what he or she is doing. Why not just do what you want to do?*

"Because that kind of thinking leads to getting your spine removed by a yeti-gator, like my dad," I mutter to myself. Like I'm going to let the voice of reason talk me down. No way. Reason is no match for my paranoia.

Then why are you here? the damn voice asks. *Why aren't you huddled away in your cabin on the* Second Chance? *Is it the girl? Are you in looove?* The idiot voice stretches the last word out into three childish syllables.

"Shut up, asshole!" I burst out. Then freeze because Greta has skipped halfway down the hall and the only person in my vicinity is Pinky. Who eyes me with a look of mild disdain.

"I didn't say anything," she says.

"No! I didn't mean you. I'd never—augh!" I plunge down the hallway after Greta, heedless of anything but putting my moronic outburst behind me.

Greta looks at me over her shoulder and smiles a sneaky sort of smile. She's skimming her hand against the wall, swooping it up high, then down low. She hones in on a door, leaning close to it and sliding her index finger across. "This one," she decides, reaching for opening mechanism.

"What's in there?" I ask.

"I don't know. Let's see." Before I can protest, she opens the door, which someone has neglected to lock, and she steps in.

I stand in the hallway, silently doing battle with the voice of reason. But Pinky catches up and nudges me forward.

As soon as I enter, I lose all sense of everything but the room itself. "Wow."

It's a data analysis center. 3D projectors provide up-to-the-second data on weather predictions, stock markets, planetary GDPs, along with thousands of other running algorithms. "Wow," I say again. I've never seen anything like it, not even in college or within the cutting-edge company I work for. "How did you know this was here?" I ask Greta, not looking at her, but at all of the machines and projecting images around me.

"I didn't." She seems bored by the room itself, but entertained by my reaction to it. "You like it?"

"It's fantastic." The room is a wonderland of facts and data and calculations. I go from one readout to the next, studying each holographic projection.

I don't know how long we've been there when Greta touches

my shoulder. Her mouth is pursed into a tiny frown. "We should go."

"Just another minute. I want to see—"

"Now," she insists, calmly but firmly.

I come to my senses. Of course, I have to follow her lead. And I do—I follow her right down the staircase and out the door of the library.

"What was that place?" I ask as we stand, looking back at the building.

"I'm sure you could look it up later and find out." Greta seems unconcerned.

"How did you know to take me—wait. I know. You didn't. Right?"

She gives me a sly smile. "Now you're catching on."

Pinky stands alongside us, saying nothing.

"So now what?" I ask.

"I showed you something. Now you show me something," Greta says.

"Like what?"

"I don't know. Just do what I did. You lead, I follow. We see what we find."

"I really can't describe what a terrible idea that is." How could I even start?

"You think every idea's terrible. Let's go." She gestures. Not in any particular direction, just a *move your ass* kind of thing.

I sigh. So, it all boils down to this. Risking my life by showing off my preposterously bad luck for two people I only met days before. But even though I about-face and begin walking, I don't feel an overwhelming sense of doom. Just a general air of doom, which is mildly refreshing.

We haven't gone half a kilometer down the sidewalk when I get a very bad feeling. Normally, I'd run away from such a feeling like a frightened gazelle. Not today. I face that feeling by planting my feet in that spot and hiding directly behind

Pinky. Because hey, I might be acting brave, but I'm not stupid.

Sure enough, in seconds, I hear a buzzing—a buzzing that grows increasingly louder, and five very long seconds later we see it: a dark, roiling cloud of bugs. What kind of bugs, I can't determine, being neither an entomologist nor a citizen of Parkorvan. But it's a big, black blob of angry buzzing, and it's coming right for us.

A yell goes up across the street, with people bolting for the nearest building. Apparently, they know what these things are, and they're not enthusiastic about this turn of events.

Do we move? Do we exercise the slightest bit of self-preservation? Nope. We stand there in the crossroads of my doom and Greta's luck, and we let Pinky's *kenogu* decide.

Greta gasps in shock and slaps a hand to her cheek. Pinky frowns and rubs at her neck. I feel a burning pinch on my forehead and realize the bugs are biters. Great. But as soon as the biting begins, and the black cloud seems about to converge on us, a massive wind comes along, scattering it. The bugs struggle against it, swirling in chaotic patterns. Greta and I grab onto Pinky as the gale force increases, threatening to knock us over.

Within ten seconds, the bug cloud disappears. Doors open and people peek to see if it's safe to come out.

"What was that?" Greta seems amazed, even though an angry red bump is rising on her cheek.

"No idea," I say, rubbing my forehead. "I hope they weren't poisonous."

"I've never seen anything like it." Greta's eyes are wide with wonder.

"So where now?" Pinky asks.

I realize I still need to lead them somewhere. Should I keep steering us wherever my danger-sense tells me not to go?

"You want to go on?" I glance at Pinky, but then focus on

Greta. This is her adventure. I don't know what she's trying to discover or prove, but maybe the bugs have scared her off.

Greta touches her cheek, gently probing the bug bite with her forefinger. She nods.

"Don't pick at it," I advise, taking her hand and holding it so she doesn't aggravate it.

She nods again, suddenly quiet. She seems fascinated with the burning pain on her face. My face burns too, and I find it far less intriguing.

I hone in again on my internal danger-meter. What feels like the worst possible choice? Ah, yes. A right turn. That feels like a terrible decision. Greta should be overjoyed with whatever comes next.

A tall, stocky man crosses the street toward us. A van-like vehicle screeches around the corner and hits the man, who bounces up onto the front of the car, then falls to the road.

I steal a look at Greta, who looks positively gobsmacked, like she's seeing Christmas for the first time. Pinky simply squints at the scene, looking undecided.

A man leaps out of the vehicle, but rather than rushing to the aid of the victim, he runs over and screams, "What the hell, man, you're not doing this to me!"

The guy on the road gets to his feet, holding one arm to his side. "Do what? You hit me!"

The vehicularly homicidal maniac only grows more enraged. "Oh, no way! I will *kill* you in self-defense! I'll do it!"

"Whatever, man." The injured guy, still holding his arm, finishes crossing the street and awkwardly opens the door to his own vehicle.

But the maniac isn't done. "Oh, no you don't!" He pulls a small capsule from his waistband and sprays something toward the other guy, who ducks and then dives into his vehicle. His tires squeal as he drives away.

The maniac notices us watching. "What?!" he screams at us, then gets back in his van and slowly drives off.

Even Pinky looks flummoxed at this point. "What was that? What just happened?"

I shrug and Greta, her mouth slightly open, merely shakes her head.

We stand there on the sidewalk, my two companions blinking and screwing up their faces in various expressions of puzzlement. I'm far less affected. I'm accustomed to bizarre circumstances in general and have developed mental armor against them. Pinky and Greta do not have this same jadedness.

"So, are we ready to head back to the spaceport?" I ask hopefully.

Pinky and Greta silently look at each other, then at me. I take that to mean that they hadn't yet grasped the reality of my existence. Fine. We'll travel onward.

I check in with my danger-sense and feel like I need to head further from the city center to find something truly deranged. I lead my friends down the parkway about a kilometer and take a right turn. At the very end of that avenue I make another right turn. After that, a left.

"It feels like we're walking in circles," Greta observes as we travel slowly down the picturesque but far less populated street.

"Nope. I promise you, something really stupid is right that way." I point, for effect. I've never tried to use my sense of doom to intentionally echolocate some crapfest of disaster. Thanks to these two, I'm acting in diametric opposition to my instincts.

Another half hour of walking leads us down a road that has no traffic at all, other than the three of us. The sidewalk ran out some ways back and now we tramp over uneven grass. I don't care for that, as the odds of my twisting an ankle or breaking a leg are too high. But it's still better than walking on the shoulder of the road. That would just be begging for a very gruesome, messy death. No, thank you very much.

Dodging Fate

When I realize we're approaching some sort of military installation, I must admit, I feel an unusually high level of trepidation. But even though my sense of self-preservation screams, *Run, you fool, or kiss your ass goodbye,* I persevere. I walk right up to the perimeter fence with Pinky and Greta on either side of me.

Nothing happens.

"Now what?" Greta asks.

"Just wait."

We wait there, with the sun shining cheerily above and happy birds chirping to each other from the trees alongside the road. And, sure enough, not five minutes later, we see something that I don't mind categorizing as epic.

A tank rolls out from behind the installation. I can't claim to know why this little university planetoid has a military base armed with tanks. Maybe they're afraid of someone coming in and kidnapping students from rich families and holding them for ransom. Or maybe space pirates have a tendency to stop off here to steal computer devices and flipflop shoes. Who knows? Maybe somewhere, there's a species of people who prize flipflops above all else.

Anyway, it's obvious that something's awry with this tank. Rather than roll out on a straight course, it weaves side to side, does lazy donuts (as much as a tank can do donuts because those bastards do not exactly corner well), and generally looks like a drunk monkey is driving it.

Comically, a squadron of uniformed officers runs out in the tank's wake, and even across the distance I can hear indistinct shouts. The officers' shouts rise an octave and they run full-out. Another tank emerges. I wonder how many of the vehicles are stored behind the building.

How does a person outside a tank stop a tank? They don't. That's the point of tanks.

I hope their guns aren't loaded.

Aha. Four more tanks deploy now, and these aren't driven

with the airy abandon of a child going, *Whee!* These newcomers drive with obvious intent toward the freewheeling pair. After some time, they manage to block the two in. Officers on the ground climb up on the rogue tanks, shouting, and, within a few minutes, they open the hatches.

A pair of monkeys clamber out.

Right. Monkeys. Driving tanks. I knew we were on the trail of something unlikely, but I hadn't expected such a spectacular show of preposterous dumbassery. There are no odds for calculating such a thing.

So engrossed is my little group in watching all this unfold, we don't notice the young, wiry human hoofing it toward us until he's within throwing distance. Since my doom-sense hasn't kicked in, I deem him a low-level threat.

"Hey!" he pants. "You shouldn't be here."

What can I say that won't make things worse? I wisely keep my mouth closed. Greta looks lost for words.

But Pinky has us covered. Though she's been quiet on this excursion, she finally roars to life, in all her glory. "Well, here we are. Outside a fence. Watching you people play war games with monkeys. What the hell is wrong with you?"

She stares the man down and he takes a half step back, stammering. "Ah, nothing's wrong with me. I'm just a PR person for the fleet."

"Then what's wrong with them?" She hitches her chin toward the tanks, monkeys, and officers. At the moment, the officers appear to be negotiating with the animals.

"Well..." he glances back over his shoulder, then returns his gaze to us. Actually, just to me. He flinches away from looking at Pinky, as if she glows with the mighty brightness of a sun. "Some lab monkeys escaped from the university. They apparently became self-aware and decided to bust up the university that had imprisoned them."

"How do you know this?" I ask.

"We have a sign language interpreter. Those are some pissed-off simians."

"I don't blame them." Greta speaks up for the first time.

The guy glances back again. "Yeah. Me either." He sighs. "I hate this job."

We all stand there, watching the monkeys and the officers gesticulating at each other. Finally, there's a long standoff. The animals seem to be waiting for something. They're handed a paper, which they confer over, and suddenly scramble down.

"It appears that the long nightmare is over," Greta observes drily.

"Will they be okay?" I ask the PR man. I feel sorry for him. He's going to have a nightmare of a PR crisis on his hands.

"Yes," he answers. "We have strict laws about sentient creatures. The university will have a lot to answer for."

I feel better about that, anyway.

"So, if you three would sign some non-disclosure agreements?" He says this as if it fits right into our conversation.

"Why should we?" Pinky asks, looking entirely indomitable.

"Well...I could offer each of you a thousand universal credits, for your trouble."

"Hush money?" Pinky closes one eye and squints at him with the other. Somehow, her glare is more concentrated and intense with just one eyeball. "I'm good with that."

She glances at Greta and me, and we readily agree. Who would believe a story like this anyway?

"Two thousand each, though," Pinky decides.

The guy licks his lips. "Sure. Sure. Two thousand." He shoves a telcoder device at us. We sign, he transfers the credits, and we're on our way.

As we head back toward the city center, I decide it's time to make an executive decision. "As interesting as this has been, it's time to get back to the *Second Chance*. We need to have these bug bites looked at, and I really don't care to have another strange run-in."

They agree to quit while we were ahead because, really, this last event is the highest note we could possibly leave on, so we go directly to the spaceport. Once inside, a doctor who happens to be traveling notices Greta's face, and dispenses excellent and free care to all three of us.

He says conversationally as he swabs our bite wounds, "Those firebug bites can be nasty. Their venom's designed to provoke an allergic reaction. You three are lucky to still be on your feet. Weird that they'd be on the mainland, though. You usually only find them on the islands."

He goes on his way, leaving me with mixed feelings. Lucky to have avoided getting caught going into a private area of the library, and to have had no major reaction to the firebugs. Maybe even for witnessing something as ridiculous as sentient monkeys driving tanks to gain their independence. Running into a doctor who wanted to treat our bites was fortunate, too. Greta's *kenogu* has been in force. But then, so has mine.

I feel unsure about how to categorize the experience. Was it an adventure or a misadventure? We all came out okay, in spite of everything.

As we enter the docking gate, Greta tries to lead some upbeat chitchat, but I'm tired and Pinky's gone back to not saying much. Greta finally falls silent and we board the *Second Chance*. The main corridor is blocked for some sort of maintenance, so Pinky leads us into an employees-only service corridor.

A sign reads, *Please remove all scuba gear beyond this point.*

"Let me guess," I say, "that means something about automatic rebreathers or something."

Pinky shakes her head at me. "No. That really does mean that employees are not permitted to wear scuba gear in the service corridors."

"Why is that even an issue?"

"It isn't, anymore. Not since we got the sign. Anyway, I'm going straight here, but you two will go left. At the next junction you can re-enter the guest corridors."

I thought I'd gotten a handle on the Garbdorian signs, but, clearly, I still haven't. Or maybe Garbdorians are just weird.

"I think I'll take a nap," Greta says when we part ways. "I'm really tired after all that."

"Facing a plague of bugs and a monkey uprising can do that," I joke lamely.

She ignores my lameness. "Want to meet for dinner?" She names a time four hours away.

"Sure. The pub, right?" I still want no part of the dining room.

"Of course." She smiles and takes her leave.

As I watch her go, I try to decide which one of us had the bigger impact on the other today.

I go back to my cabin, having made no determination.

4

You'd think the events of the day would keep me from being able to work. That I'd be preoccupied and uptight and unable to focus. But I sit down and work for two hours straight, running statistical models and showing those numbers who's boss. Somehow, I feel good. I don't mean all-my-body-parts-are-in-place-and-there's-no-yeti-gator-in-my-room good. I mean the kind of good that normal people feel. At least, I assume so.

The luck stone sits just to the right of my keyboard. I rest my index finger on it, half-believing in the thing. Stupid. It's just a rock. But still. I've survived some pretty serious events since meeting Greta.

I pick the stone up and drop it into my left palm, appreciating how smooth and cool it is. I feel like I'm in charge of my life, for the first time. Like I have options. Such as living to see middle age.

I feel different. Weird. Empowered.

Palming my luck stone, I walk to the corridor. To be honest, I kind of strut. At least it feels like a strut. It might be a mere casual stroll, but in place of my usual cautious creep, it feels pretty badass.

Tempting fate, I walk down the center of the corridor, rather than hugging close to the bulkhead. Even as I do, a shadow of my danger-sense whispers to me. What am I doing? Have I gone mad?

I squash the voice of reason in my head and blast a doot-doot-doot-da-doot-da-doot-doot kind of song over it. The kind that movie soundtracks always play when the major players show up and wow us all with their epic coolness. If I hadn't been strutting before, damn sure I'm doing it now. That's right, ladies. Take a look at all this.

I don't even pause as I approach the entrance to the dining room. I'm a new man, and I strut right the hell in.

And freeze.

The forks. So many forks. Forks in hands, forks in mouths, forks threatening to launch themselves airborne straight toward my vulnerable, vulnerable eyes.

With a squeak that is so very not badass, I literally launch myself out of the dining room. I land on the floor of the corridor and gather myself enough to crabwalk to the bulkhead and lean against it, eyes closed, my breath rasping in my ears.

Clearly, some of my deeper complexes are hanging on with a vengeance. But at least I tried. Not only had I contemplated the possibility of entering the dining room, I'd waltzed right in. It's progress. And I don't even care what Dr. Ramalama would say. I'm now convinced that my time with her was worthless. She never got me. Never understood me. She never even remembered my birthday. I mean, who spends a whole afternoon listening to someone pour their guts out, and doesn't even bother to notice that it's his birthday when it's displayed on the screen in her hands?

I rise to my feet. Screw Ramalama. She never helped me. The two people who do help are waiting for me in the pub.

We have a good time that night. We laugh, we eat, we reminisce about the sentient monkeys. We make fun of Gvertflorians and all their tentacles.

Okay, I feel bad about that one afterward. I don't consider myself better than someone with tentacles that are reflexively drawn to the groins of other species. It's just nature for them, and we're juvenile assholes to laugh about it.

But I've never had this kind of camaraderie with anyone and am swept away by the feeling. Already, I have history with Pinky and Greta, and it feels amazing.

Four days later, we visit a space station inhabited by a fish-like people that sound like they're underwater when they speak, even though the station's perfectly dry. It leads to some misunderstandings and I might have accidentally married one of them before departing.

Five days after my potential nuptials, Greta, Pinky, and I take a tour of a new Martian colony. It's rustic and new and has an air of adventure. Pinky mistakes the purpose of a particular bucket and let's just say we leave that place in a hurry.

Another five days takes us to a very basic space station with nothing to recommend it whatsoever. After so much oddness, the normalcy seems strange. Until I'm served with alimony papers from my fishwife. Apparently, I did get married, after all.

Imagine that—me, a married man. I almost feel pride at my accomplishment, but instead, I just scream and run away to the *Second Chance*.

Which brings us to Mebdar III and Greta's departure.

I feel gutted about losing her, and that isn't a fish joke. In just three weeks, she and Pinky have become my best friends. No, more than that; they've become family. The idea of living without them tears me apart inside. Normally, I'd assume I've somehow consumed a Brantaguan sea shark parasite, but I know the feeling to be dread. And heartbreak.

Our last dinner together in Pinky's pub is a somber affair. We try to keep the conversation light, but fail. Pinky and Greta seem to feel the same way I do.

Finally, Greta reaches out and puts her hand on mine. "These last weeks have been amazing. My life has always been so dull and predictable. With you two, I've seen adventure I'd never even dreamed of. I really hate the idea of getting off on Mebdar III. I'm afraid I'll do this job and when I'm done, I'll never have this again." When she says "this," she holds out her hands in a way that encompasses the three of us.

Pinky looks like she wants to say something, but instead wipes the counters with far more energy than necessary.

My heart fills, and I lean toward her to let it all spill out. To let her know how I feel.

"Yeah," I say.

Stupid, stupid constipated heart.

Greta looks disappointed, as if she expected some big words too, but she pats my hand and we sit together in silence.

"What if I don't go to Mebdar IV?" I blurt. Oh, so I do have more words in me. How about that.

Pinky stops wiping the bar and Greta watches me with hope and dread.

Greta cautiously says, "But it's safer for you there. I don't want you to get redshirted and eaten by a cyborg like your grandma."

"Not eaten, just transformed," I correct. It's an oddly common misperception. "But what if our individual *kenogus* combine to give us a new *kenogu* when we're together?"

Greta wears pure hope on her face now. "Do you think so? Like we're two sides of a magnet or something, and we neutralize each other's pull?"

Greta clearly doesn't have a strong background in science, but she gets her point across. We do seem to temper each other's luck.

"What do you think, Pinky?" I ask.

She looks from me to Greta. "I think you two are dumb if you don't stay together." She frowns. "And even dumber if you don't stay here with me."

Aw. That's practically a declaration of love, coming from Pinky.

Greta eyes me hesitantly. "So, I do this virtual tour job and then get back to the *Second Chance* before it takes off again. And you skip Mebdar IV. And we just keep going. See where our luck takes us?"

Can I do it? Give up the safety of Mebdar IV? The handrails in every room, the buffets of entirely soft, smushy foods, and the hourly health checks?

"Absolutely," I say.

Greta's eyes sparkle. "Okay, let's do it!"

I feel like celebrating. "Pinky, how about making us three Backdoor Specials?"

Pinky winks at me and heads for the blenders.

While she works, I grab one of the drink menus I've never looked at before and notice a disclaimer. *Drinks provided by provider may not always be provided.*

When Pinky returns with the massive drinks—which she somehow manages to carry in one hand—I point to the disclaimer. "What does that mean?"

Pinky tosses back half of her drink, which probably amounts to a liter of Backdoor, and I gaze at her in awe.

"It means I have the right to refuse service," she says.

"That makes sense. Who writes these terrible translations, anyway?" I ask.

"I do."

Greta and I stare at her.

"But you speak Standard perfectly," I say, puzzled.

"Yeah. I just think it's funny." Pinky shrugs.

Suddenly, my heart bursts wide open and I laugh my ass off,

right along with Greta. Eventually, Pinky joins us. We drink our Backdoors, keep laughing, and start planning our next misadventure.

I think it's going to be a good one.

ESCAPE FROM MY FISHWIFE

5

I'VE BEEN MARKED for death since my birth. Bad luck is a genetic condition among my people, and it's only due to the combined luck and badassery of my companions that I've survived this far.

This means that I'm reluctant to let my friends down. I owe them, on a cosmic level. They've taken a sectarian rube and made him into a universe-traveling adventurer.

At least, that's what I'm aiming for. Today is starting off with some hardcore training, and I'm just hoping I don't shame myself.

"Are you ready?" Deep concern shows on Greta Saltz's face.

Am I? I've been working up to this for a month.

A month doesn't feel like enough, but I don't want to disappoint Greta. Behind the bar of the *Second Chance,* Pinky looks on with the casual air of someone who isn't interested. She's good at that.

"All right," I say. "Let's do this. *Kenogu!*"

Kenogu has become our battle cry, thanks to Pinky. It's a phrase from her homeworld that translates roughly to "shit happens" but also means that it's up to you to deal with whatever's in front of you. It suits us pretty well.

Across from me, shrouded beneath a towel, lies my nemesis.

To prepare myself, I imagine I'm Pinky. Seven feet of pink Mebdarian mutant, with a constitution of what I suspect is steel if not something stronger.

Greta moves the towel aside, revealing my enemy: four long blades protrude menacingly toward me until she grips it, reverses it, and holds it out to me. "Just hold it for five seconds. That's all."

Light reflects off the monster's silver surface, gleaming at me with evil intent. I want to run almost as much as I want to impress Greta.

I'm Pinky. I'm tough, fearless, and could eat this thing if I wanted to.

I reach out and my fingers are on the handle.

I'm Pinky. I chew on razor blades for fun and sometimes grown men cry just at the sight of me.

I curl my fist around it and Greta begins counting.

"Five."

I'm Pinky.

"Four."

I once single-handedly took down a pod of bloodthirsty blagrooks, then acted like it was nothing.

"Three."

I'm not afraid of anything.

"Two."

My hand begins to shake.

"One."

I drop the fork and back away from the table. I'm not even aware of having stood up.

"Great job!" Greta cheers, rushing over to give me a hug.

Sadly, I'm too concerned with conquering my urge to dry heave to enjoy her embrace.

Pinky casually drops a towel over the fork and picks it up, then slips out the door. For someone her size, she can be amazingly stealthy.

"Thanks." My insides feel like jelly, but I'm not about to admit that to Greta. Lovely Greta with the golden glow.

Literally. She's Garbdorian, and her people have a natural luminescence. With that skin and her pale green hair, she looks wonderfully cosmopolitan to a previously Earthbound dullard like me. I've been working hard to become more like her and less of a sectarian rube. I'm making strides, but clearly there is much work yet to do.

I first boarded the *Second Chance* with nothing but tragic family history and a dream. My destination was a retirement planet, which, at the time, seemed like a brilliant place for a guy like me since I'm destined to be eaten by a yeti-gator, fall into a pulper, or be assimilated into a cyborg like my poor grandmother.

Ah, Nana. I keep meaning to write her a letter. I'm not sure how much of my real nana is left in there but she sends me a care package of shitty cookies every now and then, so there must be a little more than a glimmer at the least. And it's not her fault she makes really bad cookies. She made great ones before the cyborgs came along.

But back to forks. That's the personal phobia I've been battling for years. Dr. Ramalama, who used to be my doctor, gave me a great many sessions of unhelpful therapy for that and other anxieties.

I need to write her a letter, too, actually. I haven't yet officially fired her as my mental health practitioner. I've been gathering my thoughts. These things take time.

The truth is, Greta and Pinky have been far more help than that old ding dong ever was. Greta's bizarrely good luck has tempered my bad luck. In return, my bad luck has ensured that not everything goes her way, and she thrives on the excitement brought on by the unlikely events that come my way.

Her luck has protected me from a grisly death more than once.

We have a certain yin and yang, when it comes to luck. We balance each other out in an interesting way.

Pinky rounds out our group. Her luck is of the ordinary variety, but she has a certain terrifying badassery that is a comfort to me because I know she's got my back. It also makes me very, very careful to ensure she remains my friend.

I've landed in a sweet situation here on the *Second Chance*—it's the kind of thing that doesn't happen to a guy like me. So I've seized the day, and my kenogu, by trying to better myself.

It's an unlikely opportunity that sure beats being harpooned, like my great-granddad.

I am a lucky guy, as far as redshirts go. I have no intentions of squandering this rare good fortune.

"Let's celebrate!" Greta declares. It's early morning and we're the only ones in Pinky's bar. Statistically, I've found that fatal accidents are least likely to occur in the early morning. This is why our fork exercises take place at such an unfortunate hour. On the bright side, Pinky hardly requires any sleep, so she's game for pretty much anything.

I dig that about her.

"One yak milk for me, straight up. And a Backdoor Special for Charlie," Greta says, still speaking too loudly.

"You got it," Pinky says.

When had Pinky returned? Seriously, she has mad skills when it comes to sneaking. Who would have thought?

Pinky begins her unique, violent ballet of drink mixing. She has a way of making the process look like a vicious struggle, ending in a triumphant murder. And yet it's all somehow disturbingly beautiful.

"Care to have a drink with us, Pinky?" I hope she'll say yes and drink enough to give me some deeper insight into her. She's not terribly forthcoming, and I have a lot of questions.

She considers, then shrugs. "Why not? My mother always says, 'starting out the drunk a little day is always a good idea.'"

"Uhm." I hate to correct Pinky, but that sounded wrong. "Did you mix a couple words, there?"

"No. My mom did. Good old Mom is pretty much always at least a little bit drunk." Pinky wears an expression of pride.

I don't know what to do with that, so I ask, "So what will you drink?"

"A Peppermint Boot." She grabbed a tall, v-shaped glass.

"Peppermint schnapps, dry vodka, and beef jerky, right?" I ask.

"You got it." She turns away to make her beverage.

I sip my Backdoor. Pinky's been teaching me bartending. I still work remotely via the lightstream as a statistician, but I find I have a lot of free time and little to do with it. Learning to mix drinks seems like a good use of that time. I like how most recipes are just ratios. It suits my mathematical mind.

Plus, I enjoy hanging out with Pinky. Not only is she capable of thwarting a great many threats to my life, she's just dang cool.

Greta pats me on the shoulder. "You're doing great with the fork training."

"Thanks."

Pinky joins us with her Peppermint Boot in hand. I take a moment to appreciate the sight. Pinky keeps a selection of extra-large glassware for people who are more sizeable than most. Oh, and Martians. I always thought the jokes about them were just stereotypical nonsense, but those Martians can *drink*.

I've learned a lot during my short time in space.

Anyway, Pinky stands there across from us, holding a glass that for her is a mere beverage, but for me would constitute doomsday prepping. I'd guess that her little aperitif contains no less than three cylindrical liters of hard alcohol.

Greta sips her yak milk. For some reason, Garbdorians aren't affected by booze like most species are. It's like lemonade to them. But get some lactose in them and they're having a good time. Yak milk, for whatever reason, is especially potent for them.

I'm learning a lot about other species these days.

"You know," Pinky says after a long quaff of Peppermint Boot. "Mebdarians invented forks. So, sorry about that, since your brain is all broken and stuff."

I don't know if she's joking or serious. There's really no telling with Pinky. Her deadpan delivery has no rival. She claims her people have invented a lot of things that they definitely have not, and I think she means it. But again, it's impossible to be sure.

I've found it's easiest to just go along with it. "Not your fault. It's just a redshirt thing to have complexes and phobias."

She fixes me with a supercilious look. "Didn't say it was my fault. I said sorry your brain's broken."

Right. Okay. I lift my Backdoor at her in reply. The drink. Not the other thing. If Pinky ever decides to kick my ass, it'll be the last thing that ever happens to me.

Greta giggles. She's halfway through her yak milk and already looking happy. Her luminescence has increased, too. It's quite pretty.

My situation with Greta is tricky. I like her. Like, *like* her kind of like her. She's fun, witty, generous, and, unlike many people, not terrified to sit next to someone she knows is a redshirt. I'm rendered unable to ask her out, though, by my concern for messing up our friendship. I've never had what I have with Pinky and Greta. This level of comfort and camaraderie is otherwise unknown to me. I don't think I could give it up for anything, even a chance at more with Greta.

Plus, there's the fact that I'm married.

I never thought I'd get married. I didn't intend to, either. Greta, Pinky, and I were having some laughs on a space station run by some fish-people called the Albacore. They seemed pleasant enough, though their need to hold water in their gill pouches to keep their membranes from drying out makes them sound like they're underwater when they talk.

One of them asked me something that sounded like, "Shall

we go to the ferry?" I thought she was offering to be a tour guide. I got something way wrong, though, because a couple weeks later, I got slapped with alimony papers. I still don't understand what happened.

My wife's name is Oollooleeloo, according to the legal documents. It's kind of a nice name, actually. When no one else is in the shower room, sometimes I put my head under the water and make *Oollooleeloo!* sounds. It's fun. You should try it.

Anyway, so far I've stayed ahead of the alimony stuff. Living on a travel and tourism ship has its benefits.

That pretty much explains my life right now. It's great. The best I've ever had. I do the work for my firm, I duck my fishwife, and I hang out with Greta and Pinky. We have the most fun when the ship hits a port and we can go adventuring. Though simple days just banging around the *Second Chance* are great, too.

Greta's cheeks are turning pink, and she raises her glass for a toast. As I clink my glass against hers and Pinky's, I can only think of how much I don't want anything to come along and ruin all this.

6

As luck would have it, today we'll dock at Garvon VII. I've never been there, but Pinky and Greta tell me it's great fun. The whole planetoid is a riverfront carnival sort of thing. It's a highly popular tour destination, because who doesn't enjoy breaking up the monotony of space travel with arcade games and throwing tiny rings at impossible targets?

Every time I leave the ship, I have to give myself a stern talking-to about standing up to my phobias, pushing past the fear in my stomach, and focusing on having a good time. I need to trust in Greta's luck and Pinky's awesomeness.

And I do.

For our visit to Garvon VII, I also have to chastise myself about not mentally calculating the miniscule odds of winning any of the silly carnival games. Today will be about fun, not about statistics.

It's hard to break old habits. Especially when those habits increase the odds of my continued survival.

Back in good old cabin 25J, I get ready for the adventure ahead. I got lucky when the Chance Fleet agreed to let me rent this room indefinitely. Such a thing is typically reserved for fleet employees like Greta, as their brand ambassador, and Pinky, as their bartender. It probably helped that Greta was the one to make the request.

Do I feel bad about using her luck for my own purposes? No. Not at all. I figure the universe owes me one.

I put on a plain pair of beige shorts and an off-white shirt. Greta keeps telling me my clothes are boring, but this is another habit I've yet to break. Not standing out in a crowd and not having any decorative bits on my apparel have thus far prevented me from becoming another clothing casualty.

For my people, that's a thing.

I drop my shiny green luck stone into my pocket. Greta gave it to me, and I carry it with me everywhere I go.

As I leave my cabin, I notice the little man staying in 26J open his door. He starts out, notices me, and scowls. After a moment of visible reconsideration, he emerges anyway, eyeing me like I'm a seagull about to snatch his happy beach-day lunch right out of his hands.

I don't know what his problem is. I've never been anything but pleasant to him.

"Good morning, sir. Will you be visiting Garvon VII today?" I level a friendly smile at him.

"What if I do? Are you going to look up my nose and tell me what you see?"

I'm at a loss. That was oddly specific, and just plain weird. Maybe it's a phrase where he comes from. And now I probably look like a rube, not knowing what it means.

"Uh, no, sir, I'd never do that," I assure him.

"See that you don't!" He points at me accusingly, then stomps off down the corridor.

I probably could have handled that better, but I'm not sure how.

Nothing to do for it now. I brush off the experience and continue to Greta's quarters. She answers as soon as I knock, and joins me in the corridor. She looks happy and excited, and a little extra glowy still after her early-morning drink.

"Hi, Charlie!" she chirps. "Let's go get Pinky. I can't wait to start having some fun."

She rushes ahead at an entirely foolhardy pace. She could trip on a carpet wrinkle or be rammed by a food cart going the opposite direction at a junction. But she's wild and crazy like that.

I hurry more than I'm comfortable with to keep myself within the radius of her good luck. In my experience, the benefit outweighs the risk.

Pinky takes a full two minutes to answer her door. I wonder if she was busy and if her cabin is bigger than mine. Well, it must be, given her size. My own little space is not much bigger than a closet.

I try to peek in when she opens the door, because I'm really, really curious about what her living space looks like. For all I know, she decorates with machetes and the teeth of people who have crossed her.

But she fills the space, then closes the door behind her and the opportunity is gone.

"Let's go wreck Garvon VII." Pinky heads toward the elevators so we can disembark.

I'm both nervous and excited about how literally she might mean that.

We get in the elevator and wait for it to begin its descent. Instead, a mellow, electronic voice says, *Welcome to the Chance 3000: A new experience in elevators.*

I hadn't realized this was going to be a whole experience.

The voice continues. *We've developed the Chance 3000 to better serve you, our guests. We elevate you because you elevate us. Please enjoy your elevator experience.*

Greta looks as puzzled as I feel. Pinky looks entirely unimpressed.

State your desired destination.

"But there's only *up* and *down*." Greta says. "And since we're up, we obviously want to go down."

You said, "Up." Now going up.

"We're already up!" Greta shouts at it.

Up has already been registered. Please be patient.

"Oh, now it's getting snotty with me." One side of Greta's nose wrinkles in irritation.

She looks cute that way.

We wait for ten long, curious seconds, then the doors open.

Arrived at up. You may now depart.

"But we want to go down," I say.

You may now depart.

"No. Go *down*!" I'm getting frustrated, too.

You may now depart.

"Oh, for pete's sake," Greta says. "Let's get off and back on again. Maybe that will fix it. And no one say 'up' under any circumstances."

We do a funny little dance of leaving the elevator, then getting back on.

Welcome to the Chance 3000: A new experience in elevators.

Greta glares at the speaker that transmits the voice, but says nothing.

We've developed the Chance 3000 to better serve you, our guests. We elevate you because you elevate us. Please enjoy your elevator experience.

Not so much, at this point. But I'm afraid to even mutter something sarcastic for fear of making it do something strange.

State your desired destination.

"Down," Greta demands.

You said, "Down." Now going down.

We remain quiet as the elevator descends, all the way down to the bottom, and the doors open.

Arrived at down. You may now depart.

As soon as we're out, Greta bursts out, "That is not an improved experience! They should change it back."

"Yeah!" What my agreement lacks in words, it makes up for in supportive tone.

Then I get my first good look at Garvon VII.

Wow.

There's activity everywhere. People mill about, carnies shout to people to try their games, and costumed characters with giant heads roam about, waving and taking photos with guests.

I breathe in deeply because the scent of the place is wonderful: fried dough, popcorn, and sunscreen.

I feel instant excitement. Awe. And happiness. All things relatively foreign to me.

"What should we do first?" Greta asks.

"I want to throw some stuff," Pinky says.

"Let's go!" Greta grabs my hand and pulls me forward.

I feel light-headed. She's holding my hand. It's amazing.

Then Pinky holds my other hand and I come crashing down. Suddenly I feel weird. Like some of my internal organs have suddenly exited my body and are just lying on the pavement ahead of me.

As I look at her in confusion and amazement, Pinky gives me a big, maniacal grin.

I don't know whether to laugh or be terrified.

Before I can decide, we're standing in front of a *Throw the ball and knock down the cans* game.

You and I both know these games are rigged. Those cans are made of lead or some shit. Maybe a person can knock the one off the top, but the other two will barely even move.

I look at the cans.

I look at the carnie.

I look at Pinky.

This is going to be something special. I just know it.

"We'll take a hundred tickets." Pinky slams her thumb down

on the credit transfer device, stabs in her code, and it spits out a stream of bright-yellow paper tickets.

Just watching this is all the entertainment I could need, but then Pinky drops ten tickets on the ledge in front of her and squints expectantly at the carnie.

I feel a wave of malevolent glee that is entirely unlike me. It's just that it's so rare to get a front row look at someone nailing a swindler's ass to the wall.

The carnie smiles. He's an entirely nondescript man of nondescript origins. He could be human, or maybe something else. He could slip into the crowd and I'd never be able to describe him sufficiently for anyone to ever identify him.

Which is probably the idea.

The carnie hands Pinky a big white ball. In her hands, though, it's like a golf ball. This is the first moment when the carnie looks uncertain. His smile slips, but he puts it back into place.

"You're going to want to stand back," Pinky warns him.

"We're not allowed to leave our booths," he says. He moves as far to the right as he can, though.

"Don't say I didn't warn ya." Pinky brings the ball to her chest, winds up, and her arm flies forward.

I don't even see the ball. I see a blur of white and an explosion of cans. They fly in opposite directions, with one bouncing off the back wall with a dull *bong* sound and coming right at us.

Pinky snatches it out of the air. "I win."

She sets the can on the ledge.

By now, the carnie knows he's in the shit. "Uhm, yes, you're a winner! You can pick any of these as your prize." He gestures to a variety of stuffed animals and insanely oversized hats. He gives her time to decide, restacking the cans.

"I want to go again." Pinky looks at him expectantly.

"I...um..." The man fumbles for words. He brightens. "Hey, for such a clean shot, why don't you take one of our top prizes?"

He indicates the other grouping of items—an assortment of even larger stuffed animals.

"I want to throw." Pinky frowns at him.

He scrambles for a ball, hands it to her, and leaps over the wall to stand next to us. Behind Pinky. "You bet! Go right ahead."

She throws again. And again. Funny thing, he's not even charging her tickets now.

Finally, Pinky tires of her sport. "All right. I'll take the flamingo."

We all look at the car-sized flamingo, bright pink, smiling, with shiny eyes the size of my fists.

"What?" she says when we all look at her. "I like pink."

She doesn't seem encumbered by the thing, even as we stop to let Greta play a ringtoss game then feed the fish in the grotto. Pinky's lashed the flamingo below its legs with a rope, which she's tied around her waist like a belt. She's pulled its long wings down over her shoulders, so she can hold them with one hand.

Basically, she's giving a giant flamingo a piggyback ride.

It's almost too much for me.

I want to laugh whenever I look at her, but it feels like the wrong move. So I shove it all down, to the point that I think laughter is filling my abdominal cavity and threatening the overall health of my liver and spleen.

Greta, I think, feels the same. She looks unusually wide-eyed.

We march on, playing the carnie games, teasing one another, and laughing. Greta wins a purple hippo and little gray manatee, and, every now and then, bumps their faces together to make them kiss.

It's a little weird. But I don't say anything about that.

I don't win any prizes, but I don't stab my eyes out throwing darts at balloons, either. Which is a win for me.

Before we hit the arcades, we stop for some goodies. Pinky props her flamingo friend on a bench and sits next to it while Greta and I stand in line for sopapillas.

If you don't know what sopapillas are, and they're served somewhere on your planet, go find some. They're a kind of fried dough. They puff up with the right mix of tender flakiness and crisp friedness. Then they're sprinkled with powdered sugar and covered in honey.

I'm on the fence about whether or not the harvesting of honey equates to the enslavement of bees, but dammit, for sopapillas, I'm willing to look the other way.

I'm sorry if that makes me a monster.

Greta carries her plate, and I carry both mine and Pinky's. She and her flamingo take up a whole bench, so Greta and I sit on another.

We dig into our sopapillas. So light. So flaky. So…I take an inopportune breath and choke on the powdered sugar I've inadvertently drawn into my lungs.

I cough, aware that my mouth and cheek are sticky with honey but I can't do anything about that right now. My lungs are rebelling against the sudden attack on them.

Then Pinky's there, pounding my back. "You need another Heimlich?"

I flap an emphatic *no* with my arm. Last time she did that, I was sore for days.

"Here, drink this." Greta puts a cup of water in my hands.

I clear my throat, hard, and take a long drink.

Finally, I can breathe.

"You okay?" Greta asks, concerned.

"Yeah. I'm good." I eye my remaining sopapillas.

I decide it would be silly to let them go to waste. I'll just have to better ration my breathing.

Afterward, Pinky gets her flamingo back into place and we hit the arcades. It isn't easy. People have to make way for Pinky and her prize.

I approach a race car game. "How do these things work?"

"You've never been to an arcade?" Greta seems amazed.

That's me, the rube who's never been to one. There aren't a lot of them on Earth, and such boisterous gathering spaces have never been my thing.

I say, "No."

I fish a ticket out of my pocket. "Where does this go?"

"Oh, they take tokens," Greta says. "I'll go get some."

She sprints away before I can say anything. Pinky has lagged behind. People keep asking to take pictures with her and, surprisingly, she agrees every time. She even seems pleased about it.

I'm standing there, patiently waiting, when a familiar face comes around the racing game. I've seen this face before, although only briefly.

It's my wife, Oollooleeloo.

Her people, I suppose, are handsome in their own way. They have a roughly human shape, though their necks are as wide as their very big heads. On the sides of their necks, they have gills, which move with their breathing. Alongside their mouths, they have catfish-like whiskers.

I never meant to have a bewhiskered wife. I know it happens sometimes, but usually only after you've been married for forty or fifty years already. Starting out that way seems like a cheat.

I want to run, but she's right there, facing me. What kind of adult runs away when he comes face-to-face with a problem?

I do. Turning, and perhaps—okay, *definitely*—flailing a little, I run.

Behind me, I hear her gurgling speech, but I'm having none of it.

I see Greta as I run out of the arcade.

"What...?" she begins.

"No time!" I shout, not slowing down. "Fishwife!"

Greta's a good friend. She hears that, and she hip checks the woman beside her, moving her out of my way. Then she takes off after me.

I run down the main thoroughfare, past the carnies, past the food carts, and beyond the crowd. On the outskirts, I find a photo booth and duck in. Greta follows me in and closes the curtain behind us.

This is no ordinary photo booth. It's huge. There are costumes in here. Old-timey ones, cyborg ones, fluffy-bunny ones. The people on Garvon VII have gone next-level on their kitschy keepsakes.

"Are you okay?" Greta asks.

"Yeah. I just freaked out a little. I mean, why does she keep hunting me down? I talked to her for like two minutes."

"I don't know," Greta says slowly. "But maybe it's something good?"

I laugh, but don't feel amused. "That's your life. For me, with all of my experiences, this can only mean something bad."

She frowns. "Okay. But...what if it isn't? Your luck's been different with me, right?"

"You stepped away. I was outside your luck radius."

"I was really only ten feet away. You think that's enough distance?"

"Maybe. I don't know."

She nudges me. "So, what if it isn't something bad? Maybe it's something good. Or just something interesting?"

"How could it be? This is me we're talking about. I know I put up a good front, but the truth is, I still struggle every day. I won't even wear carpenter's pants in case the loop were to catch on something and, I don't know, pull me into a chipper-shredder or a pulper or something."

She put her arm around me. "I know you're working hard. That's why we do the fork exercises. Maybe we should work on pants next."

"Maybe. I can't think about that right now."

"Right. Your fishwife." She sighed.

"You really think it could be something not terrible?" I ask.

"Yeah. I'd like to think so. I know my experiences are different than yours, so I can't understand how hard you've had to work at things. But I respect that you've survived all that and are working so hard to overcome it. That's pretty amazing to me."

"Really?" I turn my head to look at her. How could anything I do seem amazing to her?

"Really." Her face goes all soft and smiley and her lips look so pretty. I can't look away. Help. HELP. I can't look away! I'm being weird! Oh no!

The curtain yanks back and a giant flamingo attacks us.

No. It's not an attack. The flamingo just bangs into Greta, which causes her to knock heads with me.

"You two okay?" Pinky asks. "I got here as fast as I could, but it's hard running with this thing."

In my mind, an image unfurls. Pinky, running, her long, muscular legs churning, while a giant pink flamingo bobs its head up and down with every step.

With an unmanly, high-pitched sound, I start laughing.

Greta looks startled at first, then she connects the dots and starts giggling. Then we're falling over each other, laughing hysterically, tears running down our cheeks.

I start to wind down, but Greta emits a sharp squeal and a snort that get me started again.

By the time we're done, my stomach hurts and I'm swiping my hands over my cheeks.

"You two done?" Pinky hasn't moved. She and the flamingo watch us.

"I think so." I look to Greta.

She giggles behind her hand, but nods.

"Okay," I say, trying to calm myself. "Okay." I take a deep breath. "Pinky, I have a problem with my fishwife. Should I keep avoiding her or find out what she wants?"

Pinky shrugs, which makes the flamingo nod. "Deal with it. Get it done."

Of course she'd say that.

I look from Pinky to Greta. I trust them. They'll help me. "Let's make a plan."

"WHAT PLAN IS THERE TO MAKE?" Pinky asks. She's crowded into the photo booth with Greta and me, and I keep getting whacked with a flamingo beak every time she turns to look at me. It's soft and all, but it still hurts when it hits me in the eye.

Pinky continues. "All we have to do is pick some central location. I'll stand with Mingo here, and Greta will just be there. Your wife will show up."

It might seem like not much of a plan, but I'm sure it'll work, based on Greta's luck and Pinky's sheer strength of will.

"Right," I agree. "First, though, let's get a picture made. We've never done that."

Greta nods enthusiastically. "Yes!"

Pinky shrugs and I get thwapped in the nose with a Mingo wing. "Sure."

Which, from Pinky, is practically a singing, dancing celebration.

We take our photo, and each get a copy. This will make a nice memento.

"You know," Pinky remarks as we walk along, looking for a suitable location for our fish stakeout. "Mebdarians invented photo booths."

"Mm, interesting." I try to sound convinced.

"I didn't know that," Greta says, with a synthetically bright tone.

"This looks like a good spot." Pinky stops next to a cotton candy stand and installs herself like a very large appliance.

Greta looks to one side and then the other. "Yes, this ought to do."

We're not far from the grotto, and I see a couple of human

parents holding handfuls of fish food for their little girl to drop. They're cute, in a nuclear-family sort of way.

When Oollooleeloo arrives ten minutes into our vigil, I'm not surprised. I know how Greta's luck runs.

I'm startled all the same, though, at coming face-to-face with my wife.

I wish I could read her, but I don't know anything about Albacore facial expressions. To me, she looks wide-eyed and kind of crazy. All Albacore do.

That's not me being species-ist. That's just me admitting I know nothing about them, and my frame of reference does not match up with their reality.

"Charlie," she says, sounding like she's gargling.

"Oh, hello." I'm so stupid. I ran from her thirty minutes ago like a man with his ass on fire, and then I just say, *'Oh, hello.'*

"I need to talk to you," she says.

"About what?"

She opens her mouth to speak, then notices Pinky. I guess she assumed I was standing next to some sort of display or decoration, because she stumbles backward and makes a gulping sound.

Edging away from Pinky, she says, "About our situation."

"I'm not cool with paying alimony," I blurt. "I don't even know you."

"It's not about that," she says. "If you give me a few minutes, I can explain."

It's not easy to understand her. I have to concentrate very hard, and after she's stopped speaking, it takes me a full five seconds to be reasonably certain of what she's said.

I look to Greta and Pinky, who nod.

"Okay."

Oollooleeloo points to the grotto. "Can we go over there?"

Is that outside of Greta's luck-zone? I look to her and she nods encouragingly, so I agree.

At the grotto, my wife and I lean against the rail, looking

down at the fish, who look at us, their mouths opening and closing, expecting food.

I look from them, to Oollooleeloo, and feel uncomfortable.

"I apologize for the suddenness of our nuptials," she says. "My parents have been pushing me to marry and have kids, but I don't want kids. I thought if I married a different species, they'd have to leave me alone about that. And when you seemed amenable…"

"Wait, what do you mean amenable? You asked if I wanted you to show us around, and then things somehow went very wrong."

Her semi-transparent eyelids flick closed three times in succession. I suspect this means confusion. "Show you around?"

"I thought you said, 'Should we go on the ferry?'"

She gapes at me. "I said, 'Should we get married?'"

"Why would I marry someone I just met, who I can barely understand?" I demand.

"But…I slapped you across the face."

I'm utterly confused. "Yeah, and I thought you were a jerk. That's why I slapped you back."

She puts a hand to her head. "That's an Albacore wedding ceremony. What is wrong with your people?"

"Me? Well, we don't go around hitting each other to get married, I'll tell you that! We have fancy clothes and lots of floofy words about love and forever and blah blah, then we eat cake and a few years later we sign papers to put an end to it all and pretend it never happened. Like civilized people!"

We stare at each other. We're so different, I'm not sure how we're even supposed to communicate.

"I didn't file the alimony papers," she says. "It was my parents. They took out some bad debt with people they shouldn't have, and…don't judge them too harshly. I'll take care of that so no one will bother you anymore."

"Okay. Thanks. It would be nice not to be on the hook." I

cringe. Why did I say that? What a terrible thing to say to a fish person.

She grimaces, but doesn't respond.

"So why are you here?" I ask.

"I feel guilty," she says. "I didn't realize that by marrying you, the people my parents owe money to would take an interest in you."

"Wait, what?" My eyes go to Pinky.

Oollooleeloo wrings her hands. "They said that if they aren't paid back, they will get the money from you."

"I don't have any money!"

"You don't? But you live on a tourist ship, like a bigshot."

I grip the railing harder. "Luck, mostly. I make a modest living, but nothing more."

"I am sorry." She blinks at me.

Is she? Is that what a sorry Albacore looks like?

"So people are going to come looking for me, and if I don't pay up, what then?"

"Not good things," she admits.

"How much do they want?"

"Twenty thousand credits." She hangs her head.

"What are your parents doing to get into that kind of debt?"

"Not good things," she repeats.

I wipe my hand over my face. "I'll have to figure this out. Will you be okay, Oollooleeloo?"

"Call me Oolloo. And yes, I'll be fine. Only the males in a family can be beaten to death for their relatives' misdeeds."

Oh. Well, great.

I'm glad I don't need to sit down and have dinner with my in-laws, because I don't think I'd have anything pleasant to say to them.

"I'll try to find a way to fix this. I'll check in with you soon," she says. "I'm sorry for the misunderstanding."

"Okay. Take care...I guess." I'm not sure what the standard goodbye is for one's accidental wife.

"I *will* take care." She says it with such vehemence that I think it must mean something else to her.

As she retreats into the crowd and I rejoin Greta and Pinky, I'm concerned that Oolloo and I might have had another misunderstanding.

I'M no longer in the mood to enjoy Garvon VII, so we return to the ship.

We board the elevator.

Welcome to the Chance 3000: A new experience in elevators.

Not this again.

We've developed the Chance 3000 to better serve you, our guests. We elevate you because you elevate us. Please enjoy your elevator experience. State your desired destination.

"Up!" Greta shouts at it.

You said, "Up." Now going up.

We begin to ascend and I breathe a sigh of relief. I didn't want to have a whole get-off-and-on-again thing this time.

Stopping at midpoint.

"What?" Greta blinks at the speaker. "What midpoint? There's up, there's down, and there's dangling in midair. Nobody wants to get off halfway up to the ship!"

My Uncle Victor died that way, but I don't think saying that out loud will help my companions in this situation.

State your desired destination.

"Up!" Greta's shouting now. "Up, you stupid cow! Up!"

As the elevator resumes its ascent, I hope the Chance 3000 doesn't take offense to Greta's directions.

Would you like to hear a joke?

"What?" Greta looks confused and outraged at the same time.

What do you get if you cross a human and an Albacore?

Now I'm the one who's confused and outraged. That is just hitting too close to home.

A Martian. Looks mostly human, but drinks like a fish.

Even Pinky looks taken aback by that. Insulting three species in one joke is impressive, in an appalling sort of way.

Arrived at up. You may now depart.

The doors open.

We walk back the way we came. First we drop Pinky at her cabin. She has to sling Mingo the flamingo off her back and give him a good shove to fit him through the door before going in herself. Now, Mingo takes up all the space behind her, and, once again, I am thwarted at getting a look at her living space.

"Don't worry, Charlie," she says. "We'll get all this figured out. There's something fishy about the whole thing."

Is she joking? She looks dead serious, but come on.

I merely say, "Thanks, Pinky. Goodnight."

Next, I drop Greta at her quarters.

"I hope you had fun, before the whole kneecap-breakers-might-be-after-you thing. I had a great time with you. Even the part in the photo booth was fun." She smiles, looking all glowy and wonderful.

"Yeah. Except for that end bit, I had a great time."

"We'll build on that," she assures me. "Like Pinky said. We're going to work this out. What is there that the three of us can't solve? Nothing, that's what!" She snaps her fingers.

I wish I had her confidence, but I put on a game smile.

"Thanks, Greta. I'll see you tomorrow."

I feel better as soon as I see good old 25J. But before I can go in, the man next door opens his door and peers out at me.

"You again!" He sounds so accusing.

"This is my cabin." I point to it.

"Maybe it is and maybe it isn't. Don't go getting any ideas! I pay my taxes."

His door slams.

Shaking my head, I go into my cabin. I hope that guy gets off at the ship's next stop. But my nervousness and anxiety ebb as I go through my evening routine. I've always gotten comfort from routine, and there's something about this cabin that makes me feel safe.

I hope there's some truth to that.

7

IN THE MORNING, I feel refreshed and eager for a new day. I'm not sure why. I should be riddled with anxiety about loan sharks hunting me down and making me sleep with the fishes. But I'm home on the *Second Chance,* and even if that does happen, it won't be today.

Outside my cabin, Gus hurries by. Good old Gus was one of the first people I met here, even before Greta and Pinky.

Even though he appears to be in a hurry, he stops and gives me a courteous nod. "Good morning, Mr. Kenny. How are you today?"

He refuses to use my first name or be casual in any way. He takes his job very seriously.

"Surprisingly well, thank you, Gus. How are you?"

"Fine, fine. Always a good day with the Chance Fleet. Though if you'll excuse me, I need to go see a disgruntled passenger."

"Of course, don't let me keep you. Did something happen?"

His chipper smile momentarily dims. "It's that elevator. We've been getting a lot of complaints."

I bet they are. But I say only, "Well, good luck."

"Thank you, Mr. Kenny, and have a wonderful day."

I plan on it. I'm making every day count, and not even my current situation will keep me down.

How amazing is that?

I feel so awesome about it that I decide this is the moment to write my letter to Dr. Ramalama. Now. Right this minute.

I return to my cabin, activate the lightstream, and open up the communication tool.

The spinny thing is spinning, but nothing is happening. I wait.

How long do you wait on the spinny thing before you start feeling like an asshole? For me, it's probably about a minute and a half too long. My mojo for this task starts to wane, but I fight through it.

Fine. I turn the lightstream off and back on again. Again with the spinny thing. I wait not as long this time before turning it off again.

Dammit.

I turn it on for the third time, then look for updates. Yeah, there's one that indicates I need to *click to verify all RSTLNE variables and install the GTFO update.*

I do that, then wait.

I'm not a computer guy, but I am a statistics guy and I can tell you with a ninety-nine point nine percent confidence interval that what happens next is not normal.

First, the dreaded blue screen of death. Next, a picture of a panda.

Why? Why a panda?

A pink screen. What does a pink screen mean? Or maybe it's fuschia. Is that different than regular pink?

Now a picture of…well, I'm not sure what that is. It looks like toenail clippings on a beach with the ghost of a smiling octopus in the background.

My cabin fills with the sound of cheering, clapping, and a very commercial-sounding theme song.

And then the worst happens. I mean, the absolute worst.

I'll warn you now, there's some profanity ahead.

Welcome to the Chance Lightstream 3000. A new experience in lightstream technology.

"Fuck!" I scream. "Fuckety mcfuck fuck!" My happy mood is gone.

Then I freeze in terror. What if this this is voice-activated?

But the screen creates another pop-up.

We've developed the Chance Lightstream 3000 to better serve you, our guests. We implement you because you implement us. Please enjoy your lightstream experience.

"Not bloody likely!" I say, feeling emboldened by its apparent lack of voice interface.

State your desired tool.

Is this a double entendre?

I type, *Communication.*

The spinny thing starts spinning, but I regard it with nothing but suspicion. Rightfully so, because it brings up a chatbox and tells me, *"Running search for serial killers looking for love."*

"No! Nonononono! So much no!" Frantically, I click the chatbox, and, mercifully, it closes.

I take a breath. Dare I try again?

I type, *Write a letter.*

Dictated or typed? I stare at the screen, kind of amazed that this makes sense.

Typed.

Finally, the communication tool engages, and I'm now able to write that letter of effing off to Dr. Ramalama. I mean, the notice of termination of services.

Am I even in the mood anymore? Minutes ago, I felt shiny and cheerful. Now I feel disgruntled and crabby.

Maybe that's even better.

Dear Dr. Ramalama, I begin.

I held a fork yesterday. I have two amazing friends who made that happen. *Friends who make me feel safe and accepted and gosh darn it, even interesting. They like having me around. They help me be a better person, and they don't charge me money for it either.*

I don't believe I would ever have been able to do something like hold a fork if I had remained on Earth under your care. For this reason, I am hereby informing you that you are no longer my mental healthcare physician.

I debate about the writing the next part, but if it were Greta, she'd do it. So I do.

Turns out, all I really needed was some good luck and for someone to genuinely care about me.

I sign off politely, with my full name: Charles Kenny II, Esquire.

Don't be too impressed. The *esquire* is just something passed down through my mother's family. It's not like I earned it.

On second thought, I add *P.S. Would it have killed you to remember my birthday?*

I press the *send* button before I can second-guess myself. There. It's done.

I leave my cabin again. Although I open the door slowly, my neighbor is outside and he drops to a wide-legged, arms-akimbo stance, looking at me warily.

"You again!" He glares at me.

"Yes, sir. This is my cabin. I'm your neighbor." I'm feeling too jaded at the moment to be taken aback by his behavior. Besides, I think he's crazy.

I'm unprepared for his response.

"You got nothin' on me, copper!" He takes off running. Or at least he walks rapidly with his elbows out, which I presume is what he thinks is running.

Things are getting weird around here. Is it just the universe or is it my redshirtness bleeding through?

I make my way through the ship, nodding and greeting

people I know. I carefully sidestep the dining room and arrive at Pinky's bar.

"Charlie!" Pinky calls to me. "This gentleman would like an Oblivious Flasher. Can you take care of that?"

I can't help it. I snicker.

Pinky gives me the stink eye, so I hustle behind the bar. But I'm still struggling to get hold of myself.

I turn away and begin mixing. This drink is two parts Singapore brandy (which is not from Singapore, or even from Earth for that matter) and one part iced tea.

As I set it down in front of the customer, my eyes are only on the drink. The best is yet to come. I drop in a marble-sized sphere. Its casing is instantly activated by the brandy, and for a bright, glorious moment, the whole thing lights up bright purple.

I smile to share my triumph with the customer, because an Oblivious Flasher is not an easy drink. Get it wrong, and it becomes a mere Forgetful Vagrant. And nobody orders those.

But then I freeze, because the customer is none other than my neighbor. Mr. 26J.

"Perfectly done, my good man," he says jovially. "Well done!"

What? What's happening? I look around, but Pinky doesn't appear to notice anything amiss.

"Good to meet you, son!" My addled neighbor sticks his hand out. When I nervously clasp it, he shakes my hand vigorously. "I like a man who can make a good drink."

Maybe this is the real him while the cranky man is just the result of age and dementia. I'm sad for him. He kind of reminds me of my nana. She's not herself these days, either.

"I hope you enjoy it." I mean it, too. The poor guy deserves to enjoy whatever pleasures he has left.

"I will!" The man toasts me with his glass and takes a big drink.

Pinky passes me the drink orders from the dining car. Most

are non-alcoholic, but some people, like my neighbor here, like to start the day off with a kick.

Since he isn't spitting in my eye, I decide to get a name.

"Excuse me, sir, given that we're neighbors, can I ask your name?"

"Are we?" The man looks delighted. "How nice! I'm Waldorf!" He sticks out a wrinkled hand.

I shake it. "Is that your first name or last name?"

"Only name. Why does a person need more than one? Seems excessive."

I nod agreeably. "It's nice to meet you, Waldorf. I'm Charlie." I leave off all the rest of my formal name because I don't think he'd like it.

He seems happy sipping his drink and munching on some wasabi peas. It's not my idea of breakfast, but whatever. Old people can do what they want. They've earned it.

Pinky takes the top two-thirds of the drink orders and I work on the bottom third. That gives me a Feckless Lemonade, a Morning Wakeup, and a Friendly Fishmonger to mix. That last one reminds me of Oolloo, but I can't think of her too much while concentrating on exacting recipes.

Pinky checks my work and grunts, which is glowing praise from her. A porter whisks all the drinks away.

It's a quiet morning in the bar. A lot of our guests remained on Garvon VII, and we won't onboard another large group for two days when we make our next stop.

Greta doesn't arrive until noon, which isn't unusual for her. She's a free-spirited, I-wake-up-when-I-wake-up kind of girl.

"Can I get you something?" I ask her.

"Just water, with a twist of lime," she says. "I stopped by your cabin to see if you were in it, but you weren't. So I came here."

"Boring story." Pinky joins us.

Sometimes Pinky just says whatever she thinks.

Greta notices Waldorf. "Oh, hi! Nice to see you."

Dodging Fate

He turns to peer at her. Several stools stand between them, and from the way he squints, I don't think he can see her very well. "You too, young lady."

"It's Greta," she supplies.

"Of course it is! Who else is pretty as a button like you? I'm always happy to see your smiling face."

"Are you enjoying your stay?" she asks him. As brand ambassador, she has a particular duty to be kind to the passengers. It works well since she is naturally so bighearted and cheerful.

"Oh, yes. Except I keep hearing there's a stalker around. Have you heard about it? Some skinny guy, always sneaking up on people."

Does he mean me?

"I'll make sure the captain looks into it," she assures him.

"Thank you, young lady! Now, I think I'll go see what's on the menu in the dining room." He takes his Flasher with him, moving somewhat faster than his usual shuffle.

"Are there any lushfruit muffins back there?" Greta asks.

"Yep." Pinky plucks one out of the basket and sets it on a plate. "Here you go."

"Thanks!"

I try not to stare as Greta goes through her process of tearing it up into a hundred pieces. She doesn't do this with other kinds of food. Just bread-like items.

I'm wiping down the counter when Pinky takes the towel from me.

"I'll do this," she says. "Go sit."

I mostly do whatever Pinky tells me. Don't judge. You would, too.

Pinky begins talking. "I've done some research into those Albacore loan sharks. They're bad news. They write unfair, misleading contracts, then strong-arm people into complying."

"What should I do?" I ask.

"In a week, we'll be visiting Mar de la Mar. It's a touristy, beach resort, and those sharks love the beach."

Has she been watching old detective movies? The way she said that sounded oddly familiar.

"So we'll lure them in?" Greta sounds far too excited about this plan.

"That's right." Pinky nods. "We'll stick it to 'em, and then they'll sleep with the fishes."

Yeah, she's definitely been watching detective movies.

"I think that's species-ist," Greta points out.

"Is it?" Pinky frowns.

Greta nods. "For Albacore, I think it is."

"Huh." Pinky doesn't look repentant.

"Should we still visit Perabo?" I ask. It's our next stop, and I've been looking forward to it. I enjoy all my outings with Greta and Pinky, but Perabo particularly appeals to me. It's an artist's colony. They welcome tourists who ooh and ahh over their art and love nothing more than buying things they don't need. My favorite artist, known only as Mr. Renard, sells his work exclusively at Perabo. I'd love to get a signed original, if I can afford it.

I've never been a collector, and own only a handful of items. But looking at Mr. Renard's art has always inspired me. Now that I have what I consider to be a real home, I'd like to decorate it with artwork that is worthy of it.

"Might as well," Pinky says. "Artists rarely sign contracts, so loan sharks have no reason to go there."

"Good!" Greta looks up from her plate. "I've been wanting to get back to that glass place. They make the most amazing things." She pops a bit of lushfruit muffin into her mouth and chews happily.

She points at her plate to offer me some, but I smile and shake my head. It looks like a small cake exploded, and is not the least bit appealing to me.

"Did I tell you I have a promo spot to do while we're at Mar de la Mar?" Greta asks.

I shake my head.

"It should only take a couple hours. Just a quick perfume commercial. Personally, I think the idea of it is stupid—how can a video tell you how something smells? But it must work or they wouldn't do it." Greta takes another bite of muffin.

I've always thought the same thing.

"Perfume's stupid," Pinky says.

We wait for her to say more, but she doesn't. Apparently that was her sum total opinion on the matter.

I say, "When you said you had a promo spot to do, I thought maybe it was for the new elevator system."

Greta laughs. "Nope. I'd have to work hard at saying nice things about it. I hope they get the problems worked out soon."

"Did either of you have trouble with your lightstream?" I look from one to the other, but they both shake their heads.

"Huh. Mine was trying to do something new, but it didn't work well."

"Odd," Greta says. "Usually I hear about upgrades early on, so I can tell people about them. Maybe it's a pilot program. You know, just testing it out to see what people think."

"Maybe." I can't imagine the response will be positive.

I keep them company until Greta's done eating, then excuse myself to do my work. I pray that my lightstream won't give me trouble again, and it doesn't.

For the next several hours, I lose myself in the analysis of data and trends, and make predictions based on those trends. That's my job. I love it. In all the hurly-burly of life and luck and everything that gets stuck in the corners, numbers are true, fair, and predictable. They've always helped me make sense of my world.

I stand and stretch my back. I decide to take a walk through the ship to stretch my legs and get my blood moving. A guy like me can develop deep vein thrombosis from just sitting around. And die. Just like that.

I'm glad not to find Waldorf in the corridor. I mosey to the right, past the water closet. I have fond memories of that water closet. Okay, well not exactly fond. I'm not a weirdo. But the first time I went in there, I wasn't sure of how handling certain functions in space worked, but now I'm an old pro at it. It makes me feel very cosmopolitan. The complete opposite of a sectarian rube.

I continue along this familiar path, passing both dining room and the bar, but I walk past my usual haunt. The ship's corridors are set up on a grid, so I can walk a big circle along the perimeter, as I'm doing, or turn a corner at a junction and do more of a blocky zigzag.

I continue along the perimeter. It's nice to go for a walk. I didn't do that on Earth. Too many risks and variables.

Gus turns a corner, right into my path. He's walking fast, but slows himself to something more controlled and professional when he sees me.

"Hello, Mr. Kenny. Taking a walk?"

"Yes, getting some exercise."

"Very good, sir. Don't let me keep you." And he hustles onward.

He must have something important to deal with.

I'm unusually tired. I thought the walk would perk me up, but it's only convincing me that I could use some sleep. Just a few months ago, I'd immediately suspect carbon monoxide poisoning or sudden-onset anemia. Now, I think it's more likely that I could just use an early bedtime.

After making the full circuit around the ship, I make it back to my cabin from the opposite direction. Still no sign of Waldorf. Phew.

Inside, I send messages to Pinky and Greta, telling them I'll be staying in for the evening. They won't be alarmed. My introverted nature still crops up, and I regularly spend a night in with a pack of dumplings or a pizza from the dining room and a movie.

What should I order tonight? I turn on the lightstream, hold my breath, and am relieved when I get to the daily menu without issue.

Though...the menu seems to be an issue. The dinner selections appear to be:

Big Bowl of Ice
Small Cardboard Hats for Hamsters
A Sad, Overripe Melon with an Air of Melancholy
Tiny Souls of the Damned Wrapped in a Flaky Crust
Baby Toes, Marinated in Orange Sauce
++Also available on request, a Small Bowl of Ice

Maybe this is what Gus was rushing off to handle. My guess is, there's a disgruntled member of the kitchen staff.

This doesn't help me in terms of getting food, though.

I call Greta. "Have you seen the dinner menu?"

"No, I've been catching up on some work correspondence. I've been getting a lot of new offers lately." After a pause, I hear her laugh. "I'm tempted to order the souls of the damned and the sad melon and see what happens."

"Have you heard anything about trouble with the kitchen staff?" I ask. People talk to Greta, so she tends to be in the know about such things.

"They did fire someone yesterday for eating a guest's custom meal. I'm guessing he arranged this before he left." She giggled. "Want me to go down there and see what kind of food I can rustle up for us? I was just about to order dinner, too."

"That'd be great."

"Okay. I'll let you know what I come up with!"

Ten minutes later, there's a knock at my door.

"Pizza pizza!" Greta holds two pizza boxes, but there's stuff stacked on top, too.

I move back and scrunch myself into the corner to give her a path to the table. I've already folded it down from the multipurpose furniture assembly. What my cabin lacks in space it makes up for in utilitarianism.

She slides the box off the bottom and sets it on the table.

"One Earth-style pizza for you. I also got some dumplings, since you like them."

She sets a sack on top of the box. "The head chef was so embarrassed that he kept giving me more and more food." She laughed, turning to go.

My cabin has filled with all kinds of fragrant, delicious aromas. Suddenly, I'm starving.

"Do you want to stay and eat with me?" I ask.

"Sure! I mean, if you want me to. I thought you wanted a night in or I would have asked."

"I'd love some company." I really mean *her* company, but I play it cool.

"Great." She sets her food down on the table, being careful not to let anything fall off its small surface.

She pulls a chair out of the wall and I do the same. When I first saw Gus do this furniture voodoo, I wasn't sure if I'd ever have the skill. Now here I am, an old pro.

We sit, and I realize there's a logistical problem. The food containers are already covering the table, and even hanging off in places. We're going to need plates and some room to maneuver.

"Should we put the boxes on the floor?" I ask, fearing this will mark me as a rube. Who puts food on the floor? Does this make me gross?

But Greta's a champ. "You bet. Sometimes we have to get creative out here in space. Next time we should do this in my cabin. It's just a little roomier than this, which might make it easier."

I'm momentarily stunned both by the idea that she already

wants to do this again, and that I'd get to see the inside of her cabin.

I recover when she holds my pizza box out to me. "So what's on your Garbdorian pizza?"

She leans in and takes a deep breath of it, then sighs happily. "It has a dough base, like yours, but instead of being layered with sauce, then cheese, then other stuff, it's covered in *cavalamitsi*."

She opens the lid and I'm a little afraid of what I'll see.

"It's macaroni and cheese." I stare at it.

"What?" She tugs a piece onto a plate she's removed from the interior of the box lid.

"We have that on Earth, but we call it macaroni and cheese."

"Oh. Neat. Want to try?" She offers me the slice.

"Yeah. Thanks. Want to try mine?" I lift the lid.

"I dunno." She eyes it warily. "No offense, but it's kind of weird for me."

I pull a slice of it onto my plate, next to the mac and cheese version. "How's it weird?"

She bites her lip, reluctant to answer.

"It's okay. I won't get offended."

"It's that." She indicates my favorite topping with an outstretched finger, which makes tiny, pointy circles. "It comes from such a dangerous-looking source, and it just seems strange to put on a pizza."

"It's just pineapple. It's good. See?" I take a bite and chew to prove my point.

She looks unconvinced.

"I try things every day that I instinctively feel are a bad idea. But I try them anyway." I raise my eyebrows at her.

"Ugh, you're right, I'm being a baby. Okay. Let me try Earth-style pizza with pineapple."

I put a slice on her plate, then pick up the kind she likes and take a bite.

"Mm, this is delicious." I'd have said so even if it hadn't been, but it really is.

She releases a breath, sets her jaw, and takes a bite. She chews, looking thoughtful. "It's not terrible," she says slowly. "It's kind of sweet."

"Yeah," I agree. "It goes well with the acidic tomato sauce." I finish off the slice of Garbdorian pizza, then start in on mine.

She finishes the slice, except for the crust, which she sets aside. Then she moves on to her own pizza with obvious relief.

"It's okay if you don't like it. You tried it, and that's what matters."

She smiles. "Thanks, Charlie. You're the best."

I'm sure that's not true, but Greta sure makes it sound good.

After my second slice of pizza, I eat a fist-sized dumpling and I'm stuffed.

She polishes off a third slice of pizza and reaches for the mystery bag.

"What's in there?"

"Fresh donuts!" She puts one on my plate, then one on hers.

They're all roundy and caked with cinnamon sugar.

"These look fantastic." I'm stuffed, but I bite into it anyway. Bliss! The outside has just a little bit of crunch, and the inside is so soft and cakey. "Wow. So good!"

"Right?" Greta chews, and her lips have a sandy coating of sugar. She looks adorable.

Then she sags into her chair. "I'm so full, though."

"Me too. I can't eat anything else. What do we do with all this food?"

She starts stacking it up. "I'll find it a home. There are lots of other people confused about their dining options tonight, I'm sure."

"I bet."

"This was nice." She gives me a sunny grin.

"Really nice. Thanks, Greta."

We keep eye contact for a couple beats too long, and now this feels like a drawn out moment of expectation. Like in the movies, when people kiss.

Oh, man, I'm being weird again. I just know it.

"Let me help you with these!" I finish stacking the food containers and lift them.

She stands and walks to the door with me. Well, to be precise, she has to walk to the door first, and then out into the corridor. Then I have room to follow her and hand her the food.

"I really enjoyed this. I'm glad the menu got messed up."

She laughs. "Sometimes even a mistake can be a lucky thing, right? I'm glad, too. Let's do it again soon. Goodnight, Charlie."

I lean against the door after it closes. It's so foreign to me to connect bad luck to good luck, but she's right. That's what landed me here, after all.

Kenogu.

I change into my pajamas, then convert the table and chairs into my bed. I lie down and enjoy the sensation of a full stomach, a cabin that still smells delicious, and the lingering magic of Greta's presence.

THE NEXT DAY, I am looking forward to visiting Perabo and seeing what the artist colony has to offer.

On the other hand, I have great trepidation about the elevator experience in getting there.

As Greta, Pinky, and I board, I'm tense with nervousness.

Welcome to the Chance 3000: A new experience in elevators.

I groan, bracing myself.

Now descending.

What? Greta and I blink at each other. It can't be this easy.

We descend smoothly and without interruption. No weird jokes, no threatening to return to the top, just a simple ride down.

As we step off at the bottom, I look back at it, half-expecting something dramatic to happen. It doesn't.

The ship has put us down at edge of the main thoroughfare. Each side of the street is lined with festive little shops. Some have wind chimes or streamers that flap in the gentle breeze and they range in color from sedate beige, which has a particular appeal for me, to a brilliant chartreuse that makes me a little nauseated.

I'm attracted to the little beige store, which is shaped like a little domed hut. "Should we start there?"

Pinky shrugs and Greta says, "Sure, why not?"

It's a tidy, spare little place. Even Pinky has room to maneuver without worrying about knocking anything over. The shelves along the walls are lined with small driftwood carvings.

"How cute!" Greta points to a seagull that somehow appears to be smiling. "He's so cheerful."

"A Cheerful Seagull would make a good drink name, don't you think?" I say.

"I think so. I'd try one." Greta sidesteps, scanning the shelves.

"It could work," Pinky says. "Sounds like it would be a tropical drink. I'll think about it."

"You could invent the next big fad," I suggest.

Pinky likes that idea. I can tell. Her frown is more *Hmm* than her usual *I enjoy smashing things* look.

We find many pleasing carvings, but none of us appears to be in the market to purchase one. I prefer not to own much, and surely whatever Greta wants magically appears when she wants it. At least, that's how I imagine it.

The next few shops are brightly colored and sell an assortment of decorative bottles, wall-hanging wish charms, and hand-painted miniature ships. All very interesting, but nothing I need.

I'm keeping an eye out for Mr. Renard's shop. I don't know where it's located, but each time we approach a shop, I hope this will be it.

Not this time. But Greta's delighted to have arrived at the

glassblower. We don't even notice the goods on display because we're immediately entranced by the master herself at work. She's rolling a long stick back and forth, back and forth over her work surface. At the end of the stick is, what I presume, a blob of molten glass.

I can't even count the number of ways I'd injure myself with that.

Just to be safe, I stand behind Greta as we watch. When the master gets the glass to where she wants it, she puts her mouth to the end of the long stick and blows. The bulb expands slightly. More rolling.

Apparently, rolling is a very important part of this process. The master inserts the glass into a container on the floor that has a star-shaped cut out. She blows into the stick, and when she pulls the glass out, it's now elongated, and has ridged sides.

Now that's cool.

Pinky isn't as fascinated. She's moved off to study the completed works on display.

"Charlie, which one do you like?" She's standing next to a collection of large sculptures.

Greta remains, watching the glassblower, and I join Pinky. In front of me are representations of an ocean wave, breaking high with lots of white foam, an octopus with dozens of tentacles, a ballerina, and a flower.

"The wave," I answer. "It's looks natural and fresh and free."

"Me too." She holds up her hand for a fist bump. "I'm going to check out the next place." She lowers her voice "Glass doesn't do much for me."

"Okay, we'll catch up in a few minutes."

Pinky makes a hand sign that I interpret to be something akin to *rock on* or a thumbs-up, though on Earth, what she did would be considered a very rude gesture. Especially for Italians.

Okey dokey. Put that on my *list of things that are way different out here in space.*

I return to Greta, who doesn't appear to have moved an inch. She turns to smile at me. "Neat, isn't it? I like how something can go from being one thing and transform into something completely different."

"Yeah, it's cool. Have you ever bought anything here?"

She laughs. "No. I spend almost all my time in space. Such fragile, purely decorative things aren't a good fit for my lifestyle."

"What about these?" I direct her to a counter that has a variety of small pendants. "These take up almost no space and shouldn't be too prone to breakage."

"Oh, I've never seen these. They must be new." She leans forward to study them. They're roughly oval-shaped flat discs with different patterns in them. Some are looping swirls, some seem to have suspended multi-colored pieces inside.

"Which do you like best?" I ask.

"They're all so pretty. How about you pick one for me? I'm sure that one will be my favorite."

There must be a hundred pendants. How do I choose?

I'll be methodical. First, color. Green appeals to me, because it's the color of the luck stone she gave me. There's a reciprocity about that that seems right. Okay, so green. That narrows my choices to about one-fifth of the items. Now I just need to pick the pattern. I think the swirly ones suit Greta.

I settle on a green pendant with prominent whorls. It sort of reminds me of the circles inside a tree trunk. It feels natural and organic, and suitable for Greta.

"This one." I hand it to her.

"It's perfect. Definitely my favorite." She looks so happy, I feel like I've performed some major feat.

"Do you have chains for these?" I call to the attendant behind the counter, but not too loudly because the glassblower is looking very intense about a glowing ball of glass.

"Yes, bring it over." He's a teenager with the good looks of youth. He bears a resemblance to the master, so I wonder if it's her son. "What length do you like?"

He shows Greta a variety of lengths, while I go back to the pendants and select a deep blue one with pink swirls.

While she puts her necklace on, I ask, "How much?"

"Four hundred, all together." Before Greta can protest, I whip out my account card, swipe it, enter my code, and it's paid for. I put the second pendant, which is now on a long chain, in my pocket.

"You didn't have to do that," Greta chides me.

"I know. I wanted to. You gave me my luck stone. Now I'm giving you an adventure necklace. It's fair, don't you think?"

She beams at me. Then she seems to remember something. "Oh! We'd better catch up to Pinky or we'll never find her."

"How could she be too hard to spot? She's Pinky."

"You'd be surprised," she says.

There's a story behind that, I'm sure.

We find Pinky three doors down, sitting on a bench and eating an ice cream cone.

If you've never seen a large, pink mutant eating an ice cream, let me tell you, it's entirely delightful. Every now and then, when you think she's made of nothing but acid and steel, Pinky does something wonderfully endearing.

"Look what Charlie bought me!" Greta shows Pinky her pendant.

"Pretty," Pinky says. "Where's mine?"

"Here." I take the blue one from my pocket and hold it out. "I hope you like it. I got the longest chain they had."

Pinky stares at me, her ice cream cone held aloft, but forgotten. "Really? That's for me?"

"Of course. I wouldn't forget you."

She stands and the next few moments are a blur that leave me with ice cream in my hair and a breathless feeling. But I'm pretty sure Pinky hugged me.

Then she's proudly wearing her necklace and tossing back the rest of her cone in three bites.

Which is amazing all by itself, since it was a quadruple-scoop.

We find Mr. Renard's shop, and I'm immediately drawn in. There's a subtle smell in there, like cherry pipe tobacco carried on the wind.

Then there I am, gawking at row after row of original Renard paintings.

"Robot western paintings?" Greta sounds doubtful, even though I can tell she's trying not to.

"Robot westerns are my favorite movies," I tell her without looking at her. I have eyes for nothing but all these artworks. Robots having shootouts, robots riding robot horses, and vast herds of robot cattle.

"Cool."

Pinky says, "I like 'em. Lots of laser shootouts, and all those campy sound effects." She points a finger at me. "Pew, pew, pew!"

I adopt a robotic voice. "You'd. Better. Mean it. If you. Shoot. At. Me. I will. Make you. Regret. It."

Pinky puts her 'gun' into its 'holster' and puts her hands on her hips, adopting a cocky swagger. "My targeting programs. Are superior. To yours. You. Will never. Defeat me."

We both burst into laughter. Ahh, it's like being a kid again.

"I see you two are fans." Mr. Renard stands before us, and I'm starstruck. He smiles at Greta. "How about you?"

"Oh!" Greta wears a look of panic. "I…"

Mr. Renard laughs. "It's okay not to be a fan. We're a small club."

"Your artwork is wonderfully detailed," she says. "You make it look just like a scene from a movie."

"Thank you. I'm lucky to be able to make a living doing what I love. And that I've been able to do it for so long."

I know from his biography that he's sixty-five, from one of Earth's wine country regions, and one heck of a poker player.

Not that I'm a fanboy or anything.

"Which one do you like?" he asks me. He seems to have picked me out as the one wanting to make a purchase. Clever fellow.

"I'm torn," I admit. "I love the classic shootout scenes, but I like the more pastoral, ranch landscapes, too. Like this one, with all the spaceships in the background."

"Mm. I know what you mean." He stands next to me, a finger to his lips. "You know, here's something I think you might like."

He takes a painting off the easel and leans it against the wall. Then he retrieves a pastoral scene and puts it up in its place. "See these two? Look here." He points at the facing edges of them.

The left is a shootout, the right is a field with a spaceship and a herd of robo-cows.

"They connect," I realize.

"Yes, they're a panoramic scene, but split into two. They're kind of a secret of mine. Most customers want a portable size, but my ideas are often much bigger. So I paint the whole thing, cut it down the middle, and frame them individually. I get to paint the big scenes I like, and customers get what they need."

"Clever." I don't even have to stare at the paintings and imagine them on the wall of my cabin and consider the way the light will hit them or any of that. The prices were discreetly noted below, and though they're far from inexpensive, I can afford the cost. "I'll take them."

Mr. Renard lights up. "I'm really pleased they'll stay together. I'll have my assistant box them for transport and ring them up. Do you want to come back for them?"

"That would be great. We still have some exploring to do."

Mr. Renard nods. "Good, take your time. Make sure you visit the bargain shop at the end of the row. You never know what you'll find there. For a lot of people, it's their favorite place on Perabo."

"We will. Thanks." I want to linger, but it would be weird. "We'll be back in a couple hours or so."

"Like I said, take your time." Mr. Renard waves to us.

Now what? I feel like the high point of this trip has already happened, but I try to be game. I'm still here to have a nice day with my friends.

"What would you like to do next, Pinky?" I ask.

"I wouldn't mind another ice cream cone," she says, sounding hopeful.

"Sounds good to me. Greta?"

She smiles. "Sure, who doesn't love ice cream?"

"Glavadroxavarians," Pinky answers. "Wicked lactose intolerance. You do not want to be anywhere near that."

Lactose. Right. "So, can a Garbdorian get drunk on ice cream?" I ask Greta.

"If they have enough, sure. But the sugar and other carbohydrates weaken the potency. Kind of like drinking alcohol on a full stomach for you."

"Huh. Okay."

In the ice cream shop, I'm bewildered by the vastness of the selections. There are twenty-eight flavors that can be served alone or mixed in combination with one another. There are four types of cones, waffle bowls, and plain old cups. The topping options look like a candy factory exploded.

It's a lot to take in.

Greta decides quickly on a blueberry double-scoop cake cone with no toppings. Pinky takes time weighing her options, which I wouldn't have expected since she just had an ice cream. She chooses a mere triple-scoop of lushfruit and chocolate, mixed together. Plus rainbow sprinkles. I wouldn't have pegged Pinky as a rainbow sprinkles kind of girl.

I take the longest to decide.

"A vanilla double-scoop waffle bowl, please," I say.

Greta groans. "Noooo, don't get him that. Wait one second,

please." She flashes the scoop-guy with a blinding smile and he looks momentarily stunned.

She says, "Charlie, is vanilla really your favorite? Because if it is, that's fine."

"Not really," I admit. "It just seems like the safest bet. The least likely to be gross or to have choking hazards in it."

"What sounds like it might be delicious?" she asks. "Pick something you'd really like to try."

Old habits are hard to break, but she's right.

"Okay." I look at the scoop-guy. "I'll take a double-scoop of Death by Chocolate in a waffle bowl."

"Wow, that even has the word 'death' right in it. Nice job, Charlie." Greta hits me with one of her megawatt smiles.

Even Pinky seems pleased.

It's just an ice cream order, but I feel pretty proud of myself.

We go outside to the benches and find Waldorf there, finishing off a sundae. He drops his bowl and spoon into a recycling kiosk.

"Hi, Waldorf!" Greta calls as we approach. "How was your ice cream?"

The old man considers. "I got peach passion, and I've had better. I didn't taste much passion. Though it did have a good peachy flavor, so I guess it was kind of good. And I liked how creamy it was. So, yeah, great ice cream! Glad I came!"

His rapid turnaround has me puzzled, but Greta is unperturbed. "I'm pleased you liked it. Where are you headed next?"

"Just to the pillow shop, then back to the ship. I'm getting tired."

"Have a good time!" Greta turns her attention to her cone, which is on the verge of dripping.

"You too, my dear." Waldorf waves and walks away.

We take our time enjoying our ice cream.

"Where should we go next?" Greta asks.

"I think the bargain shop," Pinky says. "It's my favorite. You never know what you'll find there."

"Okay. I like that one, too." In a blatant disregard for protocol, Greta takes a bite of her cone, even before she'd eaten her ice cream down to that point.

She's such a rebel.

Waldorf comes back into view, looking disgruntled.

"What's wrong, Waldorf?" Greta asks. "Did something go wrong at the pillow shop?"

"How did you know I was at the pillow shop?" he demands. "Are you following me?"

Greta looks gobsmacked. "No! I—"

He cuts her off, "And don't call me Waldorf! I hate when people call me that!" He stabs a finger at her, and then, for good measure, at me, and Pinky, too. He stomps off in the direction of the *Second Chance*.

Pinky just keeps eating her cone, but Greta looks amazed. She hasn't entirely adapted to the twists and oddities that fate sends my way.

"I'm so glad you two saw that," I say.

"Old fella's one planet short of a solar system," Pinky notes. "That's sad."

"I didn't realize." Greta frowns. "I'll make sure the porters know, so they can make sure he's properly looked after."

She's a good brand ambassador, that Greta.

We finish our ice cream with subdued small talk. Afterward, we head to the bargain shop.

It's larger than the other stores. Six or seven times larger, with rows of haphazardly arranged goods. Smiling cloth dolls stand next to military surplus weapons belts.

"Ooh, look." Pinky grabs a belt and slings it around her waist. She jams a pair of dolls into it, one on each side. Adopting a robot-western voice, she says, "Draw. You lily-motherboarded. Virus-laden. Scoundrel!"

I look to Greta. She hands me a belt. Okay, fine. I put it on. Greta arms me with a pair of dolls.

I say, "I. Will draw. When my subroutine. Is triggered."

It's some pretty harsh robot smack talk

We stalk around each other robotically, our hands brushing our weapons.

Pinky dashes down the next aisle, out of sight. I wheel around and rush to the opposite end of the aisle. I peek around the corner.

No Pinky. Where did she go?

"Gotcha!" Her voice is behind me. How did she do that?

I turn, but she already has dolls in her hands. "Pew pew pew!" She points the little smiling faces at me in rapid succession.

I must play the part that has been laid out for me, in long-standing robot western tradition.

I clasp my chest. "Oh! My central processing unit. Has been. Compromised." I stagger, falling back against a shelf. "Deactivat....ing."

I slump to one side and freeze.

Greta claps. Behind her, a few hesitant shoppers also clap. I guess they figure that if Greta's pleased, they might as well play along.

Maybe they think it's some sort of performance art.

Pinky's actually smiling as we return our dolls and belts to the shelf. "That was fun."

"Yeah. It was."

We don't find any other items quite as enjoyable, but we have a good time looking around and trying on some hats. Except for when we realize the things we're putting on our heads aren't hats at all. I won't say what the helpful store clerk tells us they are. Just believe me when I say that they don't belong on people's heads.

Just before we finish the last row, Greta notices some faux flowers strung to make necklaces. She plucks one off the hook and puts it on.

"Those remind me of leis," I say.

"Of what?"

"There's a beautiful island on Earth, and it's a tradition there to give arriving visitors a lei."

Pinky gives me a look.

"One of those," I point at the flower necklace.

"Less interesting, but okay." Pinky shrugs.

"That sounds nice." Greta touches the petals of one of the faux flowers. "You know, I'm going to buy all these, and give them to people who board at Mar de la Mar. We'll have a lot of new passengers coming aboard there, as they leave from their vacations. How nice would it be for the brand ambassador to give them flowers and welcome them aboard?"

She begins pulling all of the leis off the peg and draping them over her arm.

It does sound nice, actually.

We visit a few more shops, then go back to Mr. Renard's to collect my paintings. When we enter, he's there rearranging the paintings to fill in the two missing spots.

"Hello there! Mr. Corbeau has your paintings all ready to go." He ducks through a doorway and reemerges, holding a large box.

I reach for it, but Pinky reaches past me. "Better if I take this one," she says.

I'm okay with that. "Thanks."

She bumps my shoulder with her fist, very gently. "You got it."

I pay, basking for a few more minutes in Mr. Renard's presence, and then we're back on the street, returning to the ship.

This has been a great day. I'm not even mad when I hear: *Welcome to the Chance 3000: A new experience in elevators.*

Greta, holding her big bag of leis, groans.

Please select desired language.

That's new.

"Earth standard," I say and hold my breath. I fear it's going to start talking to me in clicks and beeps or something.

English standard registered. Please state favorite type of bird.
What?

"Flamingo," Pinky says.

Flamingo registered. Beginning ascent.

During the ride, I'm nervous that at any point, we will be besieged by birds. Or just bird calls piped over the audio speakers. I'm waiting for...something.

We arrive, the doors open, and that's it. No disasters have befallen us.

You may now depart. Watch out for flamingos.

"Why? What does that mean?" Greta demands.

You may now depart.

"This thing is driving me crazy!" Greta shakes her fist at the speaker, and I'm afraid it will somehow sense that and visit retribution upon us, but nothing happens.

We depart.

Greta takes her bag of leis to her cabin while Pinky carries my paintings all the way to 25J, despite my assurances that I can manage myself.

She apparently doesn't think I can.

"Thanks, Pinky." I finally get my paintings at the doorway.

"You bet. Watch out for flamingos!"

She disappears down the corridor.

IN MY CABIN, I check the lightstream for messages from work. I have lots of vacation days stored up, so it's easy for me to take a day off when we arrive at an interesting port.

No word from work, but I do have a message from Oolloo.

Alimony has been nullified. You don't have to worry about that anymore. Working to handle the debt situation with my parents. Will update you again soon.

That's good news. I'd be pleased not to come face-to-face with those loan sharks.

I really should have discussed divorce proceedings with Oolloo. I'd thought about it, but it seemed like such a personal topic for our first real conversation. The next time I talk to her, I'll definitely bring it up.

It's getting to be my normal dinner time, but I'm not hungry, thanks to all the Death by Chocolate ice cream—which, by the way, was delicious. Possibly my new favorite. The irony is kind of delicious, too.

Maybe I'll order a snack later, but I'm going to hang my paintings, and then watch my favorite robot western, *They Died with Their Datapacks On*.

Next time, I might invite Pinky to watch with me, since she's a fan, too.

Yeah, I think I will.

8

IN THE MORNING, I do a session of fork therapy with Pinky and Greta in the bar.

Afterward, Pinky and I try out a few Cheerful Seagull recipes. Greta makes the perfect test subject, since alcohol doesn't affect her.

"Too sweet," she says of my first attempt.

"Too strong," she says of Pinky's.

I reduce the amount of passionfruit and up the amount of coconut.

She takes longer before pronouncing, "It's just missing something. I don't know. It just doesn't taste cheerful."

"Maybe orange juice?" I suggest.

"Might help."

After sipping Pinky's second attempt, her lips quiver. "What was that?"

"I added some rare steak." Pinky looks hopeful. "Good?"

Greta's shoulders do a little shiver. "No, that does not make people happy."

"It makes me happy," Pinky mutters under her breath. She scoops up the glass and takes a drink. "Yeah. That's good."

"People like different things," Greta says. "Let's come up with a name for your drink."

"How about a Bloody Scream?" I suggest.

"Nah." Pinky takes a sip, looking thoughtful.

"A Raw Deal?" Greta offers.

"Nah."

I think. What would Pinky like? "A Vindictive Vampire!" I say, triumphant.

"Now that, I like." Pinky raises her glass to me and finishes it off.

Greta and I have breakfast in the bar, as we normally do, then we need to work. Greta has correspondence, and I have numbers to crunch.

"See you back here for dinner?" Greta asks me.

"I'll have to see how much work there is for me. Maybe." I'd like to say yes, definitely, I'll be here. I suspect I'll have a lot to catch up on, though. Besides, I like to keep her guessing, just a little. You know, to preserve my aura of mystery.

In the end, I do work late into the evening. Sometimes I get involved with my work and don't even realize hours have passed until my neck is cramping up from holding one position for so long.

As I'm leaning back in my chair, rolling my head from shoulder to shoulder to release the tension, I hear a clatter in the corridor.

Opening the door, I peek out.

Waldorf is there. Crap. I try to close the door quickly but not too quickly to avoid drawing his attention.

"Hey, 25J!" He calls.

Too late.

I peek out, like a turtle extending its neck outward only the barest amount.

"I dropped my tray," he explains. "Mind helping me pick it up? These old knees don't work like they used to."

He's smiling and not acting crazy, so it must be a good moment. I decide to risk it. I turn the tray over, stack up the four boxes and the bottle, and lift it. "I could carry it into your cabin, if you like."

Maybe a peek at his inner sanctum will reveal something to me.

"Oh, thank you, young man, I'll take you up on that. Otherwise, my dinner might end up being completely inedible if I drop it again." He chuckles.

He opens the door and lets me in first. As I step in, I see that his cabin is exactly like mine. His table is folded out, and the lightstream looks like it was in recent use, based on its haphazard angle.

I see a jar of muscle cream on the table, but otherwise, nothing. His few personal items must be in the storage bin, just as mine tend to be.

I put the food on the table and turn to leave. "Have a good dinner, Waldorf." I cringe. He might not want to be called that today.

"You too, young man. Charlie, isn't it?"

"Yes, it is!" I say too enthusiastically. I'm just so excited he remembered.

"Well, I won't keep you. I'm sure you have a date waiting for you. A certain green-haired girl, maybe?" Then he shrugged. "Or maybe a big pink one. Whatever you like."

"I'll probably just order a snack and finish some work."

"Wish me luck with this," he chuckled, pointing to the boxes. "I'm not sure how much will be edible."

"You can always call for room service if you need something else."

"I will. Thank you, Charlie." He smiles.

Back in my cabin, I feel sad. Waldorf is so nice when he's not suffering from one of his spells.

I determine to stop trying to avoid him. It's not his fault his mind isn't what it once was. I'll do what I can for him, for however long he's on board the ship. It is called the *Second Chance,* after all. It's a place where good things happen.

Maybe it's my newfound determination to be an instrument of good fortune, or maybe it's my pair of Renard paintings, hanging awesomely on my wall, but I spend my second evening in a row watching robot westerns until I fall asleep.

It's a nice life.

GETTING ready for a visit to Mar de la Mar gives me a mix of emotions. Greta told me to bring a swimsuit, because she's bringing hers. I don't have a swimsuit.

Redshirts take swim lessons, and then never willingly swim again. It's a survival tactic. The idea of having fun in the sun with Greta, though, has me thinking that I can buy a swimsuit at one of the shops.

As long as I don't go into the water more than ankle-deep, and Greta's with me, nothing too terrible is likely to happen. Right?

Pinky says she's working on a plan for her to lure the loan sharks out, if they're still looking for me. I like the idea of getting this situation settled, and if that's going to happen, I'll be with the best possible people to make that actually work out in my favor. On the other hand, I kind of feel like I'm throwing myself out like chum, just waiting for the monsters to arrive in the bloody, churning waters.

On the other hand...fun in the sun with Greta!

The ship lines itself up to the elevator shaft, the connections are made, and off we go.

Oh, no. The elevator.

With great trepidation, I board it, along with Pinky and Greta. I wait for the smooth voice to torture us with its unhelpful and bewildering assistance.

Instead, a man's voice comes over the speaker, screaming, "*Down!*"

The elevator descends. It is just me or is it going faster than usual?

Greta's hand is on my arm, so I don't think it's just me. I look to Pinky, who seems thoughtful.

We get to the bottom safely, though my heartrate has increased. I pat Greta's hand.

Not so long ago, she complained to me about how boring and predictable her life was, with things always going her way. She definitely can't say that now. She's getting more curveballs than a baseball game set up next to a black hole.

She smiles at me, and that gleam of adventure is in her eye. She's wearing a tiny backpack, and I'm guessing her swimsuit is in there. Then I look at Pinky and wonder what kind of swimsuit she wears.

"So what's the plan, Pinky?" I ask. This has been her department, since I have faith in her abilities for mayhem, punishment, and shaking people down. It just seems like the sort of thing that would be in her wheelhouse.

She nods as if she's been expecting me to ask. "Okay, here it is." She extends her arm toward the beach, which is still a little way off. "We go that way. At a relative speed. If people get in our way, we go around them. Unless they're the loan sharks. Then I kick their asses until they agree to leave you alone."

"That's the plan?" I expected more. A lot more.

"What more do you want?" she asks.

"I don't know. I feel like there should be more of an overall strategy. Something more, you know, strategic."

Pinky stops walking. "That sounds like a challenge."

Crap. "I didn't mean it that way."

Pinky's shaking her head. "No, it's too late. I'm totally challenged now. And I never fail to deliver on a challenge."

This feels like a bad thing to me. I peek at Greta, and it seems like she's unsure of what to make of this.

"I don't mean anything by it, Pinky. I just, you know, expected something elaborate. It's my mistake."

"Oh, no. You're not getting out of it that easily. You're going to get a plan, all right. You won't even know it when it hits you."

Right. I don't even know what that means. But Pinky's annoyed, so I go along. "I'm sure it will amazing."

"It will," she confirms.

What have I done?

"Let's change into our swimsuits," Greta suggests.

I'm grateful for her intervention. "I'll need to buy one first."

"Oh, okay. Pinky, do you have one?" Greta asks.

"I'm wearing it under my clothes." She's wearing a button-up shirt with a lushfruit print and a pair of khaki shorts. That kind of rig is apparently universal beachwear.

"Did you have something particular in mind?" Greta asks me.

"I'm not even sure of all the options. I'm thinking just basic swim trunks and a UV-proof shirt. Beige or tan or something like that."

Greta's lips twist in a funny little smile. "I had a feeling you might prefer beige. I think I know the place."

She ushers me into a cabana with only three walls. I feel a bit exposed, but I go along with it. We browse and I'm disappointed to find that swimwear on Mar de la Mar favors bright colors. I see a lot of blues and oranges and acid greens, but no beige or tan at all.

"How about this?" Greta plucks out a trunks-and-shirt combo that are a pale sky blue with some swirls of a deeper blue. Compared to the other offerings, I think this is as good as I'm going to get.

"It'll work." I grab my size and quickly pay.

Then we're at the changing cabanas. Pinky and Greta go into the unisex section, and I go past it to the men's section. I'm paranoid enough about changing in public. I prefer for it to be a gender-specific event. I know, it's small-minded. I'm working on not being such a rube. I'm just glad that there's a facility for someone like me.

After we've changed, we jam our stuff into lockers and walk down to the beach. I don't make a peep about The Plan because I already screwed that up once. I'm just going along with whatever Pinky says at this point.

I walk onto the beach in my bare feet, which Greta has assured me is the norm. I'm nervous about broken glass, jellyfish, and other horrible things, but I'm trying very hard to be cool.

She'll never know how hard I'm trying.

Anyway, we walk down the beach and I have to admit, I really like the feeling of the warm sand shifting beneath my bare feet. It's so...soft. And squishy. Like walking on piles of sugar. Very unique. I'm broadening my horizons, here, wearing blue and exposing my skin. My family wouldn't even recognize me if they saw me.

The thought makes me proud of myself. I've come a long way.

I'm usually of the cautious, creeping walk persuasion. But this burst of pride makes me loosen my gait into a free-swinging stride more akin to my fellow denizens of the beach.

That's right. Charlie Kenny's on the beach, y'all. Ready to edge into the water in my bare feet, like a badass.

Like a badass.

I hear you laughing at me. I don't even care. For my people, I am in the crazy, out-there, thrill-seeker zone. I feel like I should be wearing a red shirt that says, *I am a redshirt. This is not normal.*

A moment of epiphany comes upon me. The rush of waves in the near distance is the musical backdrop, and I can taste the salt in the air. It's like a movie moment. Not a robot movie moment, cause they'd rust like fuck in about two seconds out here. But in a feel-good kind of movie-moment way. The cries of the seagulls elongate, becoming deeper, and Greta's smile becomes almost frozen in time. Pinky's skin is bright in the glow of the sun. It's a moment that seems to last forever.

I'm going to wear red. For real. Red. The curse of my people. The bane of our existence. I will wear an actual red shirt.

I mean, not today or anything. Eventually. At some point. But I will.

Time returns to normal and I feel changed, as a person. Lighter. Better. Evolved.

Which, of course, is when everything turns to shit.

You can only push fate so far.

Time has slowed again, but not in the good, glowing, gorgeous way. It's slowed in the bad, screaming, horrible way.

Albacore men in dark suits come at us. Greta notices them, fear dawning on her face. Pinky already sees them. Her face has darkened to a deeper pink. Kind of a maroon. No, that's kind of more purply, isn't it? What I mean is magenta. That's a pinker version of red. Or maybe it's a redder version of pink.

I'm getting off point.

Even as I see these things developing, I somehow trip and fall. On nothing but sand. Because of course I do.

I land face-first into a small dune and roll down the other side. Whatever else is happening in the meantime, I have no idea because I know nothing but sand in my mouth and eyes and rolling and the heat beating down on me and the sound of seagulls in the distance.

Is this what it's like to be drunk? If it is, I will gladly continue not getting drunk, ever. Because this sucks.

I'm digressing again.

I roll to a stop on a red-and-white checked blanket, spitting out sand and trying to see. I think there's egg salad in my hair. And on my neck. I feel kind of squishy and I smell mayonnaise. When I finally get a good look, I see a flurry of pink fists and dark suits and sky and a glimpse of horrified picnickers.

It's a vast panorama of so many things. It's hard to take it all in.

I find the ground with my fists and push myself upright. Rubbing the sand out of my eyes only seems to get more sand in them. Why are beaches so popular? I can't imagine anything that sucks this much.

I hear Pinky's voice in front of me. "The forks, Charlie! Use the forks!"

What? I blindly feel around what feels like a sandwich and some soft, globby things that are either devilled eggs or eyeballs.

There's no telling what other species bring to a picnic, so I really hope they're devilled eggs.

My hands close around the plastic forks.

What do I do? I can barely see. I think of Greta.

"Kenogu!" I cry, and throw the forks.

My hand finds a bottle. Still thinking of Greta, praying it's water, I uncap it and pour it on my face to rinse my eyes.

When I can see again, I see three Albacore on the beach, lying limp. And Greta. Oh, wonderful Greta. She's descending upon me.

"Charlie, are you all right?" Her arms go around me, and she begins drying my face with something soft.

"I think so...what happened?" My vision is clearing.

"You did it! You hit those guys with the forks and they went down like a ton of tuna. I guess they're horribly allergic to plastic. And then Pinky was on them. It was terrible."

It makes no sense, but I feel so discombobulated that I sink into Greta's arms. It's the place I never thought I'd be. I might as well go with this. It's a far better way to die than I ever imagined.

But I don't die. My vision clears.

I'm getting better.

Actually, I'm just fine.

Authorities are taking away the Albacore, and my head is in Greta's lap, and holy crap, this was totally worth it.

Then I see Oolloo rushing forward, and I start to feel weird. My wife is coming, and here I am in another woman's lap.

What a great problem to have!

I sit up, but keep my arm around Greta. Because I have an excuse to.

"Charlie, are you okay?" Oolloo drops to her knees in front of me.

Do Albacore have knees? She seems to.

I suspect I've hit my head harder than I thought. Things are still coming at me in disjointed bits and confused blurs. I don't want to sound dopey in front of Greta. I want to say something that shows her I'm cool.

"I'm cool," I say.

Fucking A. I totally nailed that.

"I'm so sorry. I tried to get here sooner. My parents' debt is handled. You won't hear from those guys again." Oolloo looks worried. Her whiskers are all a-tangle.

"Groovy," I agree, feeling fine. Greta's arms are around me, and I can feel her breathing. Her nearness makes me bold. "Can we have a divorce now?" I ask Oolloo. "It's not you, it's me."

"Oh, it's me, too," Oolloo assures me. She slaps me.

"What was that for?" I roar. Actually, if I'm honest, that's probably more of a whine. But since this is my story, I'm going to characterize it as a roar.

"Slap me back," Oolloo says. "Then we'll be divorced."

"You're a violent culture, aren't you?" I say. "This would not be at all okay on Earth."

I slap her anyway.

Oolloo's whiskers wiggle and straighten themselves out. I think she's smiling at me.

"You're a good one, Charlie Kenny. I'm glad I married you."

"Uh," I say. "Likewise?"

I feel the brush of whiskers on my cheek and my wife is gone.

I am now a divorced man. Apparently. I feel instant nostalgia for all that I've lost.

It's good to have the chance to lose something and not die.

Pinky helps me to my feet. Whee, suddenly I have no weight at all. That's definitely egg salad on the back of my neck.

"You okay, Charlie?"

"Was this your plan?" I ask.

"Every bit." She says it so authoritatively, I instantly believe it.

"I may be punch-drunk from a sand dune," I say, "but you look nice in a swimsuit."

"I hear that a lot, but thanks." Pinky swings me up into her arms. "Let's get you to the medbay."

"What about our day at the beach?" I ask.

"Later."

I'm good with that. So I take a nap.

9

I WAKE UP ALONE.
I feel...different. I run my hands over my face and sit up. My cabin. I see my two Renard paintings, side by side, creating a panorama that they were secretly always meant to.
I feel good. The kaleidoscope of beachy images hits me. Loan sharks. Forks. Oolloo. A public divorce.
Oh, my god. I touched forks. *On purpose!*
Leaping out of bed, I perform a display of changing-out-of-my-pajamas-and-into-regular-clothes so swift that even I'm amazed.
Holy crap, how did I do that? It took, like, two seconds.
Never mind! I'm riding high, and seizing the moment, and making the most of it, and *all* those clichés.
I scramble down the hall to Greta's quarters. I don't even pause. I just knock.
Like a badass.
No answer, though. That's a bit of a letdown. But no matter! There are only so many places she could be on this ship.
I peek into the dining room, and there are forks, but I stare

them down. To be clear, I don't go in to the dining room but I give those forks a staring down that they won't soon forget.

No Greta, though.

When I look into Pinky's bar, though, there she is. My heart sighs in relief.

I love Greta. She may not know it, but I know it and you know it. It's our secret. For now. Hopefully, not for too much longer. I promise, I'll do my best to move this along. I'm not like other, more authoritative guys, but I know what it means to be the underdog, and I swear I will not let my unlikely fortune go in vain. I will make this count.

Stay with me.

I stride into the bar.

Greta turns and sees me. "Charlie! How are you feeling?"

"Good. I'm good."

She leaves her seat at the bar and rushes forward to hug me. I hug her back, breathing in the scent of flowers and sweetness and all that is good and Greta.

"I'm so glad." She smiles at me and kisses my cheek.

But not my cheek exactly. It's kind of further back. You know, closer to my ear. This is definitely not a *Good morning, Grandpa!* kind of peck, but a *Howdy, Sailor* kind of kiss.

Oh, yeah.

Charlie Kenny has arrived.

My heart is bursting.

Over Greta's shoulder, I see Waldorf arrive. And then arrive again.

Do I still have sand in my eyes? I pull back to rub them. But yeah. Two Waldorfs.

What the ever-loving hell?

Greta notices too, and pulls away. I keep my arm around her. Because, you know.

The Waldorfs approach the bar. Pinky wears her normal, chewing-bullets expression.

Seriously. If I hadn't fallen for Greta first, I'd have fallen for Pinky.

"Good morning," Waldorf says, sounding like Good Waldorf.

"Can I get some pancakes? And one of those Virgin Whatever-It-Was that you gave me yesterday?"

"A Virgin Cheerful Seagull?"

I shoot a look at Pinky. We hadn't yet agreed on the recipe. She raises an eyebrow at me. Okay. The recipe has been determined. I hope it's blood free.

"You got it," Pinky says. "And you?" she asks Second Waldorf.

Second Waldorf scowls at her. "I haven't liked a single thing you've made. Actually, I'm leaving. You suck!"

He stalks out, leaving us all astounded.

Well, except for Pinky. She merely looks unimpressed.

"Please excuse my brother Statler," Waldorf says. "He's always been the negative part of us. I've always been the positive. Together, we figure, we balance each other out."

Greta, Pinky, and I share a long look. *Ohhh.*

This explains a lot.

"No problem, Waldorf," Pinky says. "One Virgin Cheerful Seagull coming up, And I've ordered pancakes from the dining room. They should arrive shortly."

"That's my girl!" Waldorf praises her. "I knew I could count on you."

Amused and perplexed and not knowing quite how to feel, Greta and I join him at the bar.

That's right. My arm is still around her shoulders. We sit on stools at the bar, and only then does my arm fall to my side, but you and I know it was around her. For way longer than just a buddy-buddy sort of thing. We've gone to the next level.

I settle into place and sigh. Not a sad sort of sigh, or a disappointed sort. I'm talking more of a sigh of satisfaction. Of belonging.

There are many kinds of sighs. Don't rush to judgment on a mere expelling of breath.

Sandwiched between The Good Waldorf and Greta, with Pinky on the other side of the bar, I feel like I've arrived. I'm a redshirt who has endeavored his way into space, has been married and divorced, and who has looked death straight in the eye and thrown sand at it.

I'm a badass. Not Pinky sort of badass, but as badass as a redshirt gets.

Pinky slaps a drink in front of me. "Friendly Grandma," she announces.

I take a sip.

It's mild. It has a chicken soup sort of comforting feel, with just a hint of an astringent mothball flavor.

"Not my favorite," I admit. Still, it reminds me of my nana. I still haven't written her a letter. She may be a cyborg and all, but I think whatever part of her is still my nana would be really proud to hear of what I've accomplished.

I'm an anomaly for my people. An outlier. I've done things no other redshirt has. And survived it, too. She deserves to hear about it.

Pinky finishes off the Friendly Grandma, to my relief. Waldorf eats his pancakes. Greta happily pulverizes and eats a lushfruit muffin alongside a tall ice water. I decide to try a lushfruit muffin, too, since I'm being so darn daring.

Actually, lushfruit is a lot like pineapple. But I'm not going to tell Greta that.

She doesn't stay as long as I'd like. She has that promo to shoot down on Mar de la Mar. Pinky and I agree to come down in a few hours to meet her. Afterwards, we'll do the sightseeing and beach-going that we had intended to do before we got such a raw deal. Holy mackerel, did those loan sharks ever get schooled. Pinky cast a wide net, and then she reeled them right in. They took the bait and ended up green around the gills. That's what bottom-feeders like them deserve.

Come on, now that it's all over, I feel like we can indulge in a few fish jokes. I'm done now. I'll let you off the hook.

Okay, now I'm really done.

When I get back to 25J, I sit down and activate the lightstream. It's time to take care of something long overdue.

Dear Nana, I begin. *I have some amazing news to share.*

I pause, thinking about everything I have to tell her. There's so much, and I've never been much of a wordsmith. Maybe I should start thinking about a visit.

I pull up the *Second Chance* itinerary and start planning. As I do, my eye catches on the photo booth picture of me, Greta, and Pinky. And Pinky's flamingo.

Alone in my cabin, I laugh. Life just keeps getting better and better. Here's hoping the next chapter is even greater.

A VISIT TO MY CYBORG NANA

10

As I watch Greta Saltz, the love of my life (though she does not yet know this), I'm struck by her golden glow, her good humor, and her appalling manner of eating.

I've tried to get used to the way she decimates a hapless muffin into a pile of crumbs before eating it, but I can't. It's weird. To take a perfectly delicious-looking muffin and reduce it to hamster bedding is a crime against perfectly good food.

That muffin did nothing to deserve this kind of treatment.

But then Greta looks at me from the corner of her eye and smiles, and I know I'd forgive her anything. She could eat crackers in bed, and as long as I was there next to her, getting crackers in my crack, I'd make it work.

Even if it was the salted kind.

Not that I've even seen her bed. Or the inside of her cabin, for that matter. I've been on the *Second Chance* for months now, staring death in the face and screaming...ahem...I mean *overcoming*. Overcoming like a badass.

Yeah, that's right.

By this point, I've figured out what's what when it comes to living on an interstellar ship. How to properly use the water closet, how to get by Gus the Head Porter's scathing condescension for sectarian rubes, and even how to mix a good cocktail.

I make a fantastic Indefinite Tailpipe Twister, and my Oblivious Flashers are every bit as good as Pinky's.

I've always known that a redshirt like me can't get a girl like Greta Saltz. She's cute, fun, smart, and gosh-darn-it, people just like her. Part of it is her luck—a preternatural cosmic black hole of good fortune that comes her way. But part of it is also just Greta. She's a Garbdorian goddess, as far as I'm concerned.

Yes, I'm a dipshit for refusing to acknowledge that she's out of my league. But you know what? Screw leagues. This isn't baseball. This is my life, and for a redshirt—a guy who should have already died from a papercut or a yeti-gator or some stupid thing—I am *the man*. Charlie Kenny: a rock star among my people.

It's all relative.

As I watch Greta eat her disgustingly pre-pulverized breakfast, I'm not looking at her with rose-colored glasses, or beer goggles, or any other eyewear that's catastrophic to my life choices. I'm looking at her as a man looks at a woman who is flawed and imperfect and more beautiful to him than anything else in the universe.

That's true love, right?

"Want another Backdoor Special?" Pinky asks from behind the bar.

It's become my breakfast drink of choice, from the very first time she served me one on the very first day we met. I don't have them every morning. Only on the mornings we do fork training to help me work through that particular phobia.

Pinky is the other great love of my life. Not in the way that Greta is, though. I'm not nearly man enough to think about even being adjacent to a bed with Pinky anywhere near my relative vicinity. I'm not sure anyone is.

Actually, I really, really want to see the guy who can go toe-to-toe (literally) with Pinky and live to tell the tale. He'd have to be something amazing. Seven feet of pink Mebdarian mutant is enough to give any guy serious feelings of inadequacy.

And I know guys are her thing, so don't think I'm assuming, like some sectarian rube.

I think this is a good time to let you in on a little secret. Remember that whole affair with me and my fishwife? Being a married man and then a divorced man, and then just kind of a confused man, helped me get my priorities straight.

At least marriage is good for something.

I realized that I have a lot more life to live. Not the scuttling-under-a-rock-like-a-frightened-crab kind of a life. I mean the big picture. What I want out of life. What I want to experience before I die.

That's what made me realize how precious Greta is, and that I must cherish every day I get to spend in her presence. Ideally, I'd like that to be in the I-get-to-see-her-naked kind of way, but even if it means nothing more than being friends, I'm good with that too.

That's how much I love her. It's not about what I can put claim to. It's about what I'm lucky to receive.

Back to the secret. I meant to tell you about that, then I got distracted with Greta. It happens a lot.

Anyway, I bought a red shirt.

I know. I *know*. Don't look at me like that. I bought it, but I haven't worn it yet. Even having it folded in my tiny little storage compartment feels like I'm sitting on top of a bundle of warmth designed only for attracting a heat-seeking missile.

So don't give me a lecture about how a redshirt owning a red shirt is just begging for trouble. If anyone knows that, it's me. Seriously.

But think about it from my perspective. I'm sitting across the bar from Pinky, the baddest person who has ever been born on any plant, ever, and sitting next to Greta, the love of my life.

Can you blame me for wanting to be more than the sum of

my parts? For wanting to look death in the face and laugh? Okay, to be honest, I don't laugh. I just hide behind Pinky. But still. I'm right there, facing death, all the same, and surviving. That's a long way from the guy who intended to live out his days on a Mebdarian retirement planet.

The way I figure it, my phobia about forks, and the one about being strangled by my pants and—well, okay, all my phobias—it all comes down to me being a redshirt, right? So if I actually put that thing on, and I wear it, and I don't die...doesn't that mean I've won?

Not that today's the day. I feel like tomorrow's not the day, either. But the shirt is there, where I could even touch it if I wanted to. And my intent is in place. So one of these days...yeah. One of these days, I will face the redshirt apocalypse, and wear that red shirt, and I will survive, and it will be glorious.

Just not today. Or tomorrow. Next week doesn't look good, either.

I mean, I'm not stupid.

"I miss Waldorf," Greta sighs. "He was so sweet."

"Not like his bastard of a brother," Pinky notes. "I'm glad to get that paranoid nut off my ship. If I'd known he was disembarking, I'd have attended, just so I could kick his ass on his way off."

Greta and I pause to look at Pinky. It's a certain solidarity between us, our mutual appreciation for Pinky's take-no-shit attitude and the social discomfort that sometimes comes along with her blunt views.

I've said it before and I'll say it again: if I hadn't fallen for Greta first, I'd have fallen for Pinky.

Pinky turns away and begins her violent ballet of drink making.

I'm a little sad about our recently departed Waldorf. He and his brother have left us for Mebdar IV. Ironically, it's the retirement colony I was planning to inhabit when I first arrived on the *Second Chance*. But Waldorf will quickly become popular, I'm sure, and his brother Statler will hopefully find the right elements to keep him content in his own cranky milieu.

"Our next big port is Summadonna," Greta says between bites. "I'm trying to think of a nice boarding gift for the new guests."

As the brand ambassador of the Garbdorian Fleet, Greta has a duty to the guests of the *Second Chance*. Recently, she handed out flower necklaces as newcomers boarded, which I'd described to her as leis. That resulted in much confusion and hilarity, and she's switched to welcoming guests with more benignly named goods.

"Should we visit Summadonna?" I ask. "I've never been there."

Greta looks thoughtful. "Most of the planet is basic suburbia. Pleasant enough, but nothing special. The port, though, has a great laundromat. That's why so many people board from there."

"Really?" I can't imagine what makes a laundromat such a popular destination, but it must be pretty good. "Laundromats are really dull where I'm from. Let's check it out."

"Cool," Greta says. "It'll be fun. Pinky loves the laundromat."

"What's so great about it?" I ask Pinky.

She shrugs. "It's a chance to get out of the rut and do something different."

Maybe this is a cultural thing that humans have been doing all wrong. For us, it's a mundane necessity at best.

"I'm looking forward to it, then."

Greta looks pleased. "I didn't think you'd want to go. This will be fun." She notices the time. "Oh, I'd better run! I have a teleconference on the lightstream in five minutes." She stands, stuffing the last of her muffin crumbs into her mouth as she does.

"New job offer?" I ask. She gets them all the time. Most of them, she turns down. She only chooses the ones that sound interesting or fun.

She nods and, since her mouth is full, she strikes a bodybuilder pose, with her arms hanging in front of her, bent at the elbows, hands in fists.

"Exercise equipment?" I guess.

She shakes her head.

"Nutritional supplements," Pinky says.

Greta nods, waves, and hurries out of the bar.

"She won't take it," Pinky predicts. "She doesn't like that kind of thing. Too much of an individual-results-may-vary thing."

"Yeah. She doesn't want to rep anything that disappoints people."

"She's a peach that way." Pinky clears Greta's plate and wipes the bar.

"I like that about her, too." I finish the last sip of my drink, which is only aperitif-sized because I have work of my own to do today. "Well, I'd better get to work. Those statistics won't analyze themselves."

Pinky shrugs. She has no interest in my work.

"I'll come back to help with the dinner rush," I add. Pinky always gets inundated with drink orders from the dining room and room service that time of day.

"Sure. See you then." She doesn't turn to look at me.

I don't take it personally. I walk the long way around the corridor to my cabin, stretching my legs a bit before I sit down for hours of analytical work via the lightstream.

I crunch numbers, do regressions, and interpret results for the next eight hours. Finally, when I'm ready to join Pinky to work the dinner hour, I check my messages. My boss has been known to deliver end-of-day work that absolutely must be done immediately. He's kind of a jerk that way.

There's nothing from work, but I have received a letter from my nana.

Dear Charlie,

Received your message. The news that you are not dead is very satisfactory. I had assumed your death to be a foregone conclusion.

Your accomplishments show an adequacy previously unknown to our family.

Nana used to be like other grandmothers. She patted my head and praised even the most basic of efforts, and always had baked goods to share. Ever since the cyborgs assimilated her, she's been underwhelmingly...well, underwhelming. I realize that's repetitive, but it's the best description of her. You'll see.

She's sort of like my nana, in that she remembers her experiences and still likes baking. However, she's not the nana I once knew due to her marked lack of warmth or personality of any kind.

Nana's crazy strong now, though, and has much greater perception than us mere biological beings. I guess that's some sort of trade-off for the other things.

Anyway, back to the letter.

Given your recent improbable success, maybe you could provide me with assistance. The cyborg union has denied me a replacement for my acoustic interlink, as well as repairs on my right shoulder. These things are problematic. I either can't hear what I should, or I hear things that don't exist. My shoulder prevents normal movement. If you get back to Earth, maybe you could help me find replacements? I also wouldn't hate seeing you for a visit. I'll make you some raisin bread.

Love,

Nana

She only uses that last bit because she knows she's supposed to. I don't think she's capable of feeling love as we know it. She needs help, though, and she's still my nana. Why the cyborg union goes around assimilating hapless grannies and then not giving them proper maintenance, I don't know.

If I'm lucky, she'll forget her promise of raisin bread. Nana used to be a first-rate cook, but everything she makes now comes out tasting like robot ass. I prefer not to think about why.

I pull up the current itinerary of the *Second Chance*. We're already on a course back to Earth, so visiting Nana is a no-brainer. First we've got the stop at Summadonna, then on to Mars. From there we'll be full-on to Earth.

A certain ambivalence comes over me. Earth is home, and home is always a good thing. On the other hand, my entire life on Earth was one of anxiety and bad luck. If it weren't for Nana needing help, I don't think I'd even leave the ship during that stopover.

But what kind of guy doesn't help his ailing nana, even if she is a cyborg? I don't really have a choice here.

That means after the laundromat and Mars, Charlie Kenny will be making his triumphant return to Earth.

11

"Going back home, huh?" Pinky jiggles the hell out of a silver cocktail shaker, looking more like she's murdering the thing than mixing a drink.

"Yeah." I've explained to her my nana's plight, and am hoping she'll offer to help. I'll need her and Greta both if I'm going to make this work.

"I've never visited Earth," Pinky muses as she pours a Cheerful Seagull into a glass and garnishes it with an orange slice. "I guess I could check it out with you. You can show me some sights after we help out your grandma."

If sightseeing is the price I must pay for Pinky's help, then that's what I'll do. "Sure. We can get some funnel cake."

"Funnel what?" Pinky's looking at me like I've suggested we lick filth off the floor.

"Cake. It's a fried dough. They put sugar on it. It's good."

"Oh, fried dough. Mebdarians invented that. I like it."

Pinky thinks her people invented a lot of things. I just agree with her because it's easier.

I'm mixing a Mendacious Moocow, and I can't remember the

proportions. "Is it one part rum and two parts coconut milk, or the other way around?"

"Trick question. It can be either. It just depends on how it was ordered."

I squint at the drink order. "It just says Mendacious Moocow."

"Two parts coconut milk. But if it's a Mad Mendacious Moocow, then you flip the proportions, and add four drops of cayenne sauce."

I shudder at the thought of what that must taste like.

"Have you heard from Greta?" I ask. "She usually shows up around now."

"She said she's ordering room service in tonight. She has some emergency voiceover work to do."

As I mix the Moocow, I wonder at what would constitute an emergency for voiceover work. I come up with nothing, except maybe the person who was supposed to do the job fell through and they were on a deadline or something.

Regardless, if the job went to Greta, it must be a lucky break. That's the only kind of break she gets.

I was looking forward to seeing her, but I decide I'll take room service in my cabin, too. It's been a couple weeks since I watched movies and went to bed early. I'm due for some robot western fun. I'd invite Pinky to watch with me since she's also a fan of the genre, but she'll be tending bar most of the night.

Besides, it will give me a chance to write Nana back and let her know that soon, her grandson will be coming for a visit.

WE'VE ARRIVED AT SUMMADONNA. The *Second Chance* has connected to the elevator down to the planet, and I'm going to meet Pinky and Greta to check out this amazing laundromat.

I'm left with a dilemma. I only have a few outfits, and I send out my clothes every two days to the cleaning service on the ship.

I don't have much to wash. But who shows up at a laundromat without stuff to launder? With a feeling of desperation, I put my one dirty outfit into my duffle bag, then add all my clean ones, too. Even the swimsuit I bought for the time we went to Mar de la Mar.

On second thought, I remove all of my underwear from the bag. I don't want Greta looking at them. It's weird.

But wait. If I don't have underwear, wouldn't *that* be weird? She might think I don't wear them or something. So which is more gross? Her seeing my underwear and presuming they're dirty, or her thinking I'm a freeballing, take-my-chances kind of guy?

This is complicated.

I stuff the underwear at the bottom of the bag, then put the other clothes on top. This way, I can delay the final decision until we get there. Maybe there will be some clue to help me decide.

My hand grazes the red shirt and I eye it, like a robot cowboy sizing up the enemy during a duel.

Nope. Today is not the day. I close the door to my storage compartment.

You win this one, red shirt. But there will come a day when we do battle and I win.

Pinky and Greta are at the elevator when I arrive. I feel the situation begin to go sideways when I see how they're dressed.

Greta's wearing glittery bright-pink shorts and a neon-green halter top that's so vivid I feel my pupils dilating. Her pale-green hair is up in two ponytails, and she's tied pink and green ribbons into them. Her makeup is strangely sparkly, and, combined with the natural gentle luminescence of her skin, she's so shiny that I keep blinking.

She's also wearing the green swirled-glass necklace I bought her. Aw.

Pinky's wearing turquoise pants with a thick black stripe down the outside of each leg. She's also sporting a tank top that shows off her bulging biceps and her womanly assets in a way that makes me cover my eyes altogether.

"Are you okay, Charlie?"

I peek through my fingers to see Greta peering at me with concern. "I, uh, got something in my eye. Ow."

I put on a show of rubbing my eyes, then blinking rapidly. "I think I got it."

They're both carrying smallish bags. I guess I overpacked on the laundry front.

Pinky asks, "Where are your clothes for the laundromat?"

I pat my duffel bag. "In here."

She nods. "Gotcha."

I feel a little better. They must be wearing weird clothes because it's laundry day and everything else is being washed. Maybe those bags of theirs are bigger on the inside.

My anxiety ebbs. Until I hear a familiar, unwelcome, automated voice.

Welcome to the Chance 3000: A new experience in elevators.

Greta and I groan.

"I thought they fixed this," I complain.

"Shh! It'll hear you!" Her eyes widen with panic.

We've developed the Chance 3000 to better serve you, our guests. We elevate you because you elevate us. Please enjoy your elevator experience.

We remain silent.

State your desired destination.

"Down," Greta says.

You said, "Down." Now going down.

Greta and I exchange a look of relief. The Chance 3000 has given us troubles in the past, but maybe Gus got all of that sorted out.

Stopping for a moment of contemplation.

"Who's contemplating?" Greta whispers to me. "It or us?"

"I don't know," I murmur, helpless. "Let's just quietly contemplate something and see if that does the trick."

"What do we contemplate?" she whispers.

I don't know. I look at Pinky and say the first word that comes to mind. "Flamingos."

Pinky gives me a thumbs-up. She likes flamingos.

Concluding contemplation. Continuing to down.

I hold my breath. Hopefully we can continue unmolested from this point.

Stopping for dance party.

"What?" Greta's face is a study of confusion that reminds me of the first time I tried to use the water closet in space.

Commence dancing.

A fast bass beat fills the elevator with an *oonf oonf oonf oonf* sound. And now there are strobe lights. I throw a perplexed look to Greta and Pinky.

Pinky is not one to panic. She shrugs and begins stepping from side to side, pumping her fists in the air.

She's surprisingly good.

Greta drops low and starts doing some sort of movement that makes her behind bounce around like a bowling ball in a paint shaker.

I didn't know a booty could do that.

The space-time continuum seems to shatter around me. Everything goes white.

Then Pinky's heavy hand on my shoulder reminds me that I'm supposed to be dancing. I shuffle awkwardly to the left, then to the right, and raise my hands, willing them to do something cool. Something manly that says, *Hey, ladies, I'm a man of the universe.*

They flap like dead chicken feet.

Fuck. I don't know how to dance.

But the Chance 3000 seems to be satisfied. The music shuts off and the lights stop.

Nice moves. Proceeding to destination.

I hold my breath until we get to the bottom.

Arrived at down. Please depart.

Usually, I ascribe to the idea of ladies first, but I get my ass off that elevator faster than I even knew I could move.

Since the elevator is a direct link to our destination, I immediately get a good look at it.

This place doesn't look like any laundromat I've ever seen. We seem to be in a large atrium, like the ones at huge concert halls where people mill about when waiting for the big event to open up. Visitors stream in and out of a huge pair of double-story doors.

Everyone's dressed in bright colors like Greta and Pinky. I see glitter, fringe, and—in one case—a guy wearing chaps.

Popular misconception: there's no such thing as assless chaps. All chaps are, by design, assless. Chaps with an ass in them would be regular old pants. But it's entirely accurate to say that the fellow wearing them did not have pants on under his chaps, and my day was turning out to feature a lot more ass than I'd anticipated.

This couldn't be coincidence. All these people couldn't be so bizarrely dressed because all their other clothes were dirty.

I ask, "What is this place?"

Greta looks at me, puzzled. "The laundromat."

"I don't think it is."

"It is," she assures me. "This is the best laundromat in the galaxy."

"Okay, so define 'laundromat.'"

A little frown forms between her eyebrows. "You know, a place where people dress up, and dance, and there's lots of nakedness and drugs and stuff. A regular laundromat."

"That's not what a laundromat is on Earth."

"Oh." Greta looks all cute and serious. "So what is it on your planet?"

"It's a place where you go to wash dirty clothes. And get them clean. And dry. You know. Laundry."

"Ohhhhhhhh." Greta now understands my confusion. "No, this is different than that."

"Right." Here I am, at a nightclub with the woman I love, carrying a bag full of my supposedly dirty underwear.

Pinky's eyes fall on my duffel bag. "So that means that's not an awesome outfit. It must be…"

"My laundry," I admit.

Pinky takes it from me. "Don't worry, Charlie. I'll put it in a locker for you. Go on in, and I'll catch up."

I notice she's also wearing the necklace I bought for her, and it makes me feel better. If Pinky values something I gave her, I must not be a completely useless sectarian rube. "Okay."

"We'll have fun." Pinky pats my shoulder and disappears.

She is ridiculously stealthy.

Greta grabs my hand and pulls me through the giant doors. I don't know what to expect, but I'm pretty sure whatever happens won't be good.

It's not that I'm a negative person. That's just statistical probability.

I follow her in, though. Both because it's Greta and because her luck bends statistical probability the other way. That makes this endeavor a total crapshoot.

The place is as big as a warehouse and full of loud music, gyrating bodies, and a weird smell I decide not to think about too hard.

As I'm looking around, a guy walks up. He's a tall, good-looking Garbdorian and only has eyes for Greta. "Want to dance?"

She hooks her arm around mine, resting her other hand on the inside of my elbow. "Thanks, but I'm with someone."

I know she means as a friend, but that doesn't stop me from feeling a rush of pleasure.

My warm fuzzies dissipate when the guy asks, "Who?" Like she isn't standing there with her hands on me. As if I'm invisible.

Greta only smiles. "The best." With a little tug, she leads me away. Once we get some distance, she asks, "Want to dance?"

I'm about to say no when the fast song playing segues into a slow song. Normally, I'd say no to dancing because, as you already know from my sad performance in the elevator, I can't dance. But slow dancing is nothing more than standing across from someone with your hands on them and swaying a little.

Even I can do that.

"Sure," I agree.

She beams at me and leads me into the middle of the crowd. I can't count how many couples we pass. I don't care. They're just scenery to me.

She picks her spot and puts her hands on my shoulders. I put my hands on her waist. Then we sway.

It's nice.

"I'm glad we came here," Greta says.

"Me too."

"Life has been so much more interesting since I met you."

"I can say, without reservation, that the past several months have been the best in my life." There's no comparison. The times I've had with Pinky and Greta have been amazing.

We stop talking and enjoying the swaying for a while, but then we have a lot of eye contact and the silence starts to feel awkward. I need to say something.

"How has your work been going?"

"Good. Actually, I just landed a small part in a movie. It'll only take me a day to do, and I'll be able to get it out of the way when we drop by Mars on the way to Earth."

"That sounds exciting." I've never seen a movie set.

"Yeah. I've always wanted to do a movie. Just for the experience of it. You should come and watch the filming."

"Think that'd be okay?"

She nods and her hair ribbons flutter. "Yes, I already asked."

"Great."

All too soon, the music ends, changing again to a fast, driving beat. I step back, my arms falling to my sides.

She looks uncertain. "You don't want to dance anymore?"

I look down at my feet. "Well, I just don't know how to dance to music like this."

The guy from before butts in, putting his hand on Greta's arm. "Looks like your friend wants to sit this one out. How about you dance with me?"

I'm not happy about this, and I can tell that Greta isn't, either. She hesitates. This is where I should step in on her behalf, but I'm just not the kind of guy who steps up and makes a scene.

Fortunately, Pinky is. She appears and her arm slides around the fool. Since I never got his name, I'm going to just call him Guy.

Anyway, she hugs him in tight to her side. "I am dying to dance! Thank goodness someone else here is, too!"

"I never knew you liked dancing so much," I say.

Pinky lifts her chin. "Oh, yeah. I'm the best. Galaxy class."

Guy looks frightened. Good.

Pinky takes him by the hand and clears a wide swath. Apparently, her dancing requires a lot of room.

Then she breaks out the moves, and I realize she wasn't kidding. She's incredible. She's got her hips swaying and footwork going, and her posture is fantastic. She spins Guy out, pulls him back in, and strikes a dramatic pose with one finger pointing straight up. Then she pulls Guy back in and propels him around the entire space she's cleared.

Most people have stopped to watch at this point. Some are just staring in amazement, others clap to the beat and call out encouragement.

Guy doesn't look like he's having fun. He should be. Pinky's making him look like a total dance pro. She picks him up for a fancy lift move, then swings him back down to his feet. And on they go with more footwork, working the dance floor.

When the song finally ends, the crowd erupts in applause and whistles.

Everyone else is looking at Pinky, so I'm the only one who sees Guy running for his life.

The music starts back up, and people drift away to do their own dancing or mingling or whatever.

"That was awesome, Pinky. You're a very dynamic dancer."

She seems pleased. "Thanks. Want me to teach you some moves?"

Do I?

I peek at Greta, who nods.

"I guess? Just something basic I can do in a situation like this. Nothing fancy. I'm not very coordinated."

"Nonsense," Pinky argues. "Anyone can dance. It's just a matter of doing a little practice so you don't look stupid."

Encouraging but blunt. I never have to wonder what Pinky really thinks.

She leads me through a sidestep thing, showing me what to do with my arms so they don't look like dead chicken feet or pinwheels or something. Then she shows me how to step forward and back.

"If you just do that, changing the pattern, no one will notice you can't really dance. They'll just see you moving. And after you've done this a while and gotten comfortable with it, you can add in some more things." She moves so easily, she makes even these basic steps look really good.

"Thanks, Pinky. For the dancing and for making that Garbdorian guy buzz off."

"Buzz off?" She starts looking around. "Did he go? Damn. He was a good dance partner. Limber. I like that."

"Kind of a jerk, though," Greta points out.

"Well, there's that," Pinky admits. "But if he was nice, I'd have felt bad about swinging him so hard. So it worked out."

"I guess it did." Greta seems pleased even though Pinky looks disappointed to have lost her partner.

We shuffle through a few songs. Well, I shuffle. My friends look great. They're the best dancers in the place, in my opinion.

"Should we get some punch?" I ask. "Or some food? I saw a refreshment table over there."

Greta's eyes widen. "Oh, no. You never eat or drink at a place like this, unless you want to go flying so high you won't come down for a week. Literally, a whole week."

"Oh. Well, let's not do that."

"Don't put on any stickers, either," Pinky warns.

"Okay." I was unlikely to do that anyway, but it's good to know. "Oh, and don't accept any chewing gum."

"Right." I think I've got this place figured out. "Don't put anything in my mouth or let anything touch my skin."

Pinky looks thoughtful. "Yeah, that should pretty much cover it."

After a shuffling through a few more songs, I feel thirsty. "So what am I supposed to drink down here? I could use something cold."

"There's a bar next door." Pinky stands up straight. "Want to go?"

"I was thinking about just a water or something, but yeah, if that's where we need to go."

"I could use something, too." Greta somehow looks as fresh as she did when we first arrived.

After an hour of close confines in a warm space, I feel kind of sweaty and smelly. Walking back out through the big double doors is some relief, as the temperature immediately drops a few degrees.

We follow a walkway, then enter a bar. It's not like other bars I've been to.

Pinky's place, for example, has barstools, plus some tables and chairs. Mostly, it has drinks. It's a nice enough watering hole, but Pinky hasn't gone out of her way to give it a decorative ambience. That's what I think of as a bar.

But the place we've entered is different. It's bright white, with orange, red, and yellow décor. The feeling of the place is super cheerful. I see what looks like a milkshake mixer and some other odd equipment I've never seen in a typical bar. Actually, this looks more like a sundae shop.

"What kind of place is this?" I ask.

"It's an ice cream bar." Pinky gives me a weird look, like I should know that ice cream bars are always adjacent to laundromats that are actually discotheques.

I'll just roll with this one. "Right! Great."

I hope I can still get some water.

Pinky orders an actual ice cream bar, size extra large. I've never seen frozen novelties come in a variety of sizes, so I'm curious to see this. The bartender comes out carrying Pinky's dessert with both arms. He's lifting with his knees, but his back is rounded and his shoulders are hunched forward.

That is one big ice cream bar.

With an immense look of happiness, Pinky sits at a high table near the door and begins chomping.

Greta orders a sundae with just about every topping they have. Which is a lot. When the cup comes out, I can't even see any ice cream under there. I see gobs of candy covered with oozing toppings.

I love her, but her eating habits are gross.

I choose chocolate ice cream with cherry boba. If you've never seen boba, they're little candy bubbles that break when you bite them and release some liquid candy. They're yummy.

As if it has only just occurred to me, before I turn away with my ice cream, I ask, "Oh, you don't happen to have water, do you?"

The bartender serves me a large cup of water.

I totally nailed that.

Pleased with my success, I sit down with Pinky and Greta and begin eating my ice cream. After a couple of bites, I notice how big Pinky's bites are. I mean, they're huge. If I ate that much ice cream that fast, I'd get a—

"Ooh," Pinky says, clapping her palm to her forehead.

"Brain freeze?" I ask sympathetically.

"Yeah." Her face is scrunched up for several seconds before she opens her eyes and gives her head a shake. "Awesome."

She resumes her rapid ice cream consumption. I guess she likes brain freezes.

Greta is the last to finish her treat. She scoops up the last bite, then sits back and sighs. "That was yummy. Now what?"

"Why don't you two go back to dancing? This has been fun, but I think I'm going to go back to my cabin."

Greta brightens. "I didn't want to say anything, but I'm tired. I'll come back with you."

We look at Pinky.

"I'm not leaving. I have a lot of dancing to do. I'll see you two tomorrow." With that, she chucks her napkin in the recycling vac and boogies out of the shop. Literally. She's dancing as she goes.

I admire her confidence so damn much.

As we walk back to the elevator, Greta hooks her arm around mine, like she did before. It's nice. Fewer people are moving through the atrium, so either the party is as hot as it gets, or people have gone somewhere to sleep. Or whatever they do after visiting the laundromat.

"What do you think the Chance 3000 will have in store for us this time?" I ask.

"I'm not sure how it could top the dance party."

"What do you think all that elevator nonsense is about?"

"I haven't wanted to say anything, but..." she glances around quickly, as if worried someone might overhear. "I think Pinky did it. It has her sense of humor all over it."

"Really? Can she do something that complex?" I wouldn't have expected programming to be in her wheelhouse.

"I've found that there is very little Pinky isn't capable of. And she loves punking people. I'd have to say she's the most interesting person I've ever met." Greta smiles.

"I'd say you and she are tied, for me. You're both pretty amazing. I'm lucky to have found such good company."

She gives my arm a jiggle. "Don't sell yourself short. You're the second most interesting person I've met."

"Me? That can't be true. You've met tons of people. I'm just a statistician with statistically unlikely bad luck."

We've arrived at the elevator. It opens and we step on. I hold my breath.

Welcome to the Chance 3000: A new experience in elevators. State your desired destination.

"Up," I say.

You said, "Up." Now going up.

I let out the breath I was holding, and Greta goes the same.

She turns to face me. "Really, Charlie. You're a great guy. The bravest person I know. You'll try anything, and you're kind to people. It would be really easy for you to be bitter about what life has handed you, but you're so nice. You even help Pinky out at the bar. It's inspiring."

Wow. I consider myself kind of a sad sack, but she makes me sound really great. And she means it.

Her gaze burns bright with sincerity, and she's grasped my hands with hers. We're looking into each others' eyes and *oh my god, we're having a moment*. Not just awkwardness, but an actual *moment*. I feel like I should confess how fantastic she is, but she moves a little closer and I wait to see what she's going to do, hoping it's what I think she's going to do.

Activating night vision mode.

What? No!

We've plunged into darkness, except everything's gone green. Instead of just having pale green hair, Greta's now all green. Except for her eyes, which are little black holes in her face.

"Charlie?" Greta's voice sounds anxious and her hands grasp more tightly to mine.

"It's okay. Just stand still." I put one hand on her waist to help steady her.

"Right. Thanks."

We're silent until the elevator stops.

Arrived at up. Enjoy your stay on the Second Chance.

If I could punch an elevator in the face, I would.

The doors open and Greta and I gratefully step onto the ship. I've lost her hands in the process, and grabbing them again now would be weird.

The moment is lost. But it happened. You saw it.

I walk her to her cabin. She stifles a yawn behind her hand. "Wow, I'm really tired."

At her door, we pause, and rather than our usual easy camaraderie, there's a definite awkwardness.

Is that good? Does that mean there's some chemistry going on here? Or does it mean things have gotten screwed up? I have no frame of reference for these things.

She smiles and says, "Do you want to come to my cabin for dinner tomorrow? We said we'd watch a movie together sometime."

I restrain myself from expressing the rabid enthusiasm that fills me. "Yeah, that would be great."

Smooth. So freakin' smooth.

"Good! I'll see you tomorrow." She disappears into her cabin and I'm left standing in the corridor, staring at the door, like a dingus.

I don't care, because I'm a dingus who has a date with Greta Saltz.

Dodging Fate

I'M GOING to level with you. You've been with me since I left Earth, back when I was expecting to quietly live out my days on a Mebdarian retirement planet. So I feel like I owe you some honesty for sticking with me for so long.

I've never been on a date.

Yes, there was that one time I hung out while girls were present, but mostly they were having fun with my classmates while I went home early to avoid being pulled into their youthful hijinks.

Hijinks and redshirts do not go to together, let me assure you.

So dating is new to me, and I just don't have the experience I'd like to have in this regard. I need advice. Some wise guidance from someone who's blunt as hell and will tell me what I really need to know.

Pinky is the only possible choice.

When I arrive at the bar that morning, she takes one look at me, comes around the bar, and then closes the place. It's like she knows.

She sits in a chair in the middle of her sanctum and makes an I'm-gonna-make-you-an-offer-you-can't-refuse gesture, directing me to the chair next to her. She sprawls comfortably, with one arm on the chair back and the other resting on the table.

"Tell me about it," she says.

I have a very weird sensation, like if I do this right, I'll be a made man, and if I do it wrong, I'll wake up with a horse head in my bed. Those are some pretty wide extremes, so naturally, I clam up.

My palms sweat. My heart races. I can't figure out how to start.

Pinky's seen me at my worst. That time when I almost choked to death on a tater tot comes to mind. She knows who I am and where I'm from. This shouldn't be so hard.

She makes a small wave of the hand, a gesture that says she's got this covered. "Okay. I'll start, then."

A tsunami of relief crashes over me. Pinky gets me.

"This may sound strange," she begins, "but it's all completely normal."

Oh, good. Whew. Normal. I like normal. Right smack-dab in the center of a normal distribution, with no outliers, no need for even thinking about standard deviations because here we are, smack-dab in the middle of *completely normal*.

Pinky nods, wearing a look of sympathy. "When two people are attracted to each other, biological forces come into play."

That's a weird way to start, but dating has a lot to do with a person's natural makeup of attraction and interest, so I'm prepared to ride this out with Pinky. See where she's going with it. Surely there's some wisdom once she gets to the point.

"The details depend, of course, on the anatomy of the two people. Or maybe more than two, if you're Gvertflorians or some of the other species who…"

Her voice becomes an odd sort of buzzing. I think my brain has shorted out. I'm pretty sure this conversation has gone a very wrong way, and I'm afraid to tune back in. But a date with Greta hangs in the balance, so I focus on tuning out the static and listening to Pinky.

"…penis."

Oh, no, good galaxies, no. I just…I can't. I can't listen to the birds and the bees, with Pinky's very blunt and galactically cosmopolitan twist.

This isn't what I signed up for.

"…might seem a little weird…"

I'm on my feet, and I don't remember standing up. "I..uh…" My brain searches wildly for some excuse. Any reason to leave the room. All of the cells in my body are telling me that escape is the only option at this point.

"Combustion!" I yell. I'm not sure where that came from.

"Freakin' bats!" Don't know where that came from either. I think my brain has reverted to some Neolithic sort of self-preservation.

I run away. There is absolutely zero thought process involved. This is not a conscious choice, so don't judge me. It's like when you shield your eyes from bright light. This is pure, inborn instinct.

When I'm capable of processing my surroundings again, I realize I'm in the water closet near my cabin. Why here? I don't need to pee.

Oh, hell. I run my hands over the front of my pants.

No. No, I'm good.

I lean against the cool wall by the sink and try to make sense of it all. I'm like a person post-blackout-drunk, trying to remember what happened the night before. Trying to pinpoint the moment where it all went wrong.

"Charlie? You okay?" Pinky's voice echoes off the hard surfaces of the water closet.

"Yeah. Good. Fine." I try to make my voice sound deep. I don't really know why.

"Are you sick?"

"No. I just...uh..."

Pinky comes into view, big and strong as ever, but with a soft look of concern. It's the concern that undoes me.

"I freaked out a little," I admit. "I wasn't looking for a sex talk. I just wanted some advice on how to make a date nice. For Greta."

Pinky frowns. "Well, when I go on a date, I always like—"

I sense this going into a bad territory again, so I cut her off. "Just a date. Like, first date. Innocent. Nice. No penises involved."

Oh my god, did I actually say that?

But Pinky brightens. "Ohhh, I get it. Right. Sorry about that. I misunderstood."

My whole body sags with relief.

"You sure you aren't sick?" she asks.

"No. I'm just, uhm, you know."

"Lame," she concludes sympathetically.

"Yeah." Fine. I'm lame. Pinky gets it. I'm good with that.

"I think I went at this the wrong way," she says.

This makes me feel better. "Yeah?"

She nods. "Yeah. Let's get out of the toilet and go talk in your cabin."

As far as I'm concerned, those are some pretty golden words. "Yeah. Okay. It's this way." I lead her out and to 25J, the place I call home.

It's only when we're both standing there that I consider Pinky's mass versus the maximum capacity of my tiny cabin.

Whatever. Physics be damned.

I go in and fold down a pair of chairs from the multipurpose furniture assembly that's so cleverly built into the wall.

I sit and gesture to the other chair, which Pinky eyes warily.

"I haven't sat in something like that since the blagrook incident of '94," she says. Then she shrugs. "Whatever. Go with the flow, right?"

"I've been trying to," I agree. "Ever since I came aboard here."

"Right." She looks like she's thinking deep thoughts. "Right."

I feel like she's going to come to some kind of point or logic or conclusion or something, so I just sit and wait.

"So here's the thing," she says. "Dates are nothing. Not even a thing."

"How's that possible?" I ask. "Human culture is practically engineered around the concept of dating."

"Well that's stupid," Pinky says, dismissing my species' entire way of life. "Dating means people hanging out together, spending time. That's it. You and I do that all the time."

"Yeah, but it's different."

"Not really," she argues. "We hang out together because we like it, right?"

"Yeah," I admit.

"And you're nice to me and I'm nice to you, because we like each other, right?"

"Yeah, but—"

"But balls," she says.

I feel like that must be a phrase where she comes from because she says it so authoritatively.

"That's all dating is," Pinky insists. "Two people who like each other, hanging out, and not being assholes to each other. What's hard about that?"

"When you put it that way, it sounds easy," I admit. "But when it's you and me, there's no wondering if there's going to be, you know, something more."

"Like pressing squishy bits together?"

I don't know if she means kissing or other stuff, but either way, I do not want to pursue the thought further. "Sort of. Just intimacy in general, you know? How do you know if someone's interested?"

"Ahhh." Pinky nods in an I-understand-everything-now kind of way. "You don't know when you should up the ante."

"Exactly." Finally, she understands.

"For a guy like you, it's easy. Just wait. Let her up the ante."

It can't be that simple. "Don't women like a guy who takes charge?"

"Sometimes. Sometimes not. That's a highly complex concept, and, frankly, you're not up to it. So, for you, the best approach is to wait for her."

"I don't want to be passive," I say. "I have feelings. Strong ones. I don't want her to think I'm just..."

"Lame?"

I didn't mind when she said it the first time, but now she's kind of rubbing me the wrong way. "I don't want her to think I lack interest or passion. I want her to know that my feelings are strong, and that I want to face whatever the galaxy brings, with her."

Pinky squints at me and purses her mouth, nodding slowly. I wish I knew what this means.

"I get you," she says. "I get where you're coming from. Pay close attention to her. Let her make the first move, but when she does, you move in and close the deal. The last thing you want to do with Greta is leave her hanging. Got it?"

"I think so?" I understand what she's said, but I'm not sure how to connect this to a real-life situation. "How do I recognize a move?"

Pinky presses her lips together and makes a deep "Hmmm," sound. She seems to be taking the question seriously. "That might be tricky. Greta is by nature an open, honest, and happy person. There have been times that people assumed an interest when she was only being friendly."

"Am I doing that?" I ask. "Is she only being friendly?"

"I don't think so." Pinky frowns. "She's different with you. She's been extremely happy since meeting you, too. I think you've given her variety and excitement. I think she's actually interested."

I blink at her several times. I suspected that my date with Greta was a real date, but to have it confirmed by someone as realistic as Pinky is something else altogether.

"Wow," is all I can say.

"Yeah." Pinky's tone is all agreement. "So don't screw this up, pal, or you'll regret it forever."

Well, that's quite a pep talk. Instead of feeling invigorated, I feel the spectre of the grim reaper on my shoulder.

She slaps my knee lightly. "Don't look so serious. Just be yourself. Natural. Have fun with her. If you two are right, it'll happen."

I feel better about that. "Thanks, Pinky."

"You got it, pal."

We sit in companionable silence for a moment. It's just long enough for me to notice how ridiculously outsized Pinky is for my teeny little cabin. She looks like a basketball player sitting on a preschooler's chair. If she were to yawn and stretch, she'd probably punch out my lightstream.

"What are your quarters like?" I ask.

"Bigger," she says. "Pinker. And way cooler. Although," she looks thoughtful for a moment, "your Renard paintings are awesome."

I look to my pair of robot-western paintings, and I'm proud of them. Not just because Pinky thinks they're cool, but because I thought they were and I bought them from the artist himself. To me, they are a symbol of my entire adventure in space.

"I'd better go reopen the bar. People get pissy when they want a drink and can't get one."

"I'll come help," I say.

Pinky holds up a staying hand. "Nah. You hang out. Think about your plan for the evening. Think about just having a good time, and going with whatever happens. Get yourself in the right headspace."

"Right. Thanks."

She gives me a gentle pound on the shoulder as she unfolds herself from the chair. "No problem. Just remember to name your first kid after me, if you ever have one."

Truth be told, I think about that for a long time before I switch to getting myself into a go-with-the-flow headspace.

12

WHEN I GET to Greta's cabin, she's wearing a pale-green dress that stops just above her knee. It's cute and sexy and modest all at the same time, and is just so very Greta, because she's all good things at once, too.

She's ordered pizza for us, both Earth-style and Garbdorian-style, and we both have some of each while chatting about this and that. Then we watch a movie—some Garbdorian romance, which is a little far-fetched but has enough humor to keep me interested.

We chat. We eat. Briefly, during the movie, she shifts and her shoulder is against mine. It's nice.

I'd like to be able to describe some epic scene where we declare our love and one thing leads to another and suddenly there are fireworks and rockets and other thinly veiled imagery. But it's just a very nice evening, and I'm not sorry. A mere pleasant evening with the woman I love is more than I ever hoped to get out of life.

Our fingers don't brush one another, and I we don't get into some big tickle fight that becomes a whole romantic interlude. But I'm in her cabin, which is about twice the size of mine and decorated in sunny yellows and oranges, and I feel like she's really let me into her life for the first time.

It's a beginning, and that's an amazing thing.

Afterward, she sees me off at the door, and we have a moment of awkwardness after saying goodnight.

"I'll see you tomorrow, then," I say, ducking my head to hide my uncertainty.

"Okay. We can have breakfast at Pinky's." Her eyes are big and beautiful, and I feel like she's kind of inviting me to kiss her, but I heed Pinky's warning.

I wait.

Greta's smile suddenly brightens into a grin and she steps closer, then kisses my cheek. "Goodnight, Charlie." She looks at me from under her lashes, looking so happy, and I know this is not a chaste sort of kiss. It is an opening salvo kind of kiss.

"Goodnight," I say as the door closes.

I owe Pinky one. She was right. Any other guy would have kissed Greta first. But not me. I'm the one guy who wouldn't, and that means I'm the one who tempted Greta to kiss him first.

I am *the man*.

And Pinky's a genius.

IN THE MORNING, I wake, dress, and feel like this is a new beginning for me. I pass right by the dining room, forks and all, and don't even hurry my step. When I get to Pinky's, Greta's already inside, eating a waffle sandwich.

It's a Greta thing. It's two waffles with eggs and sausages and chocolate chips inside, and all the innards have been coated with candied sweet potatoes. The kitchen makes them special for her, and good thing, because I think the mere sweetness factor would choke most people.

"Yep. I have a real appetite this morning." She takes a big bite, which smears her cheeks with orange.

Pinky shoots a look at me but I do an it-wasn't-me shrug. Pinky squints at me hard before returning my shrug.

"Maybe it's this upcoming movie role," Greta muses after a sip of her juice.

"What are you playing?" Pinky asks as she mixes a drink.

"Oh, it's nothing." Greta looks embarrassed. "It's just a little walk-on role. The lead of the movie has just broken up with his girlfriend and as he walks off into the crowd, he bumps into me. He says, 'Excuse me,' and I say 'Don't worry about it,' and then the movie ends."

"Shouldn't take too long then, I guess," Pinky says. She sets a plate of eggs and potatoes in front of me. Apparently, that's what I'm having for breakfast today.

I've found it's easier to just let Pinky give me what she thinks I want. She's usually right.

Greta chuckles. "No, it'll just be a few hours of shooting. It's nothing. I just think it would be fun to be on a movie set."

I eat quickly and excuse myself to get to work. I'd taken the previous day off to mentally prepare myself for my date with Greta, so I'll have a lot to keep me busy.

After slaving the day away with statistical analyses, I order my dinner to my cabin and plan to watch a movie. Or part of one, anyway. Just enough of the beginning to help me fall asleep. I've always found it pleasant to drift off with the sound of robot cowboys defending their territory in the background.

To my surprise, Gus himself delivers my dinner. Gus is the head of service on the *Second Chance* and not just some porter. He doesn't handle food. When I see him outside my door holding a tray, though, I immediately suspect something is amiss.

"Here's your dinner, Mr. Kenny. I hope you'll find it satisfactory."

"I always do, Gus," I assure him. "Your kitchen staff is stellar."

He gives me a tight little bow and looks to one side, then the other, with a furtive look. Something is definitely going on here.

"Is there something I can help you with?" I ask.

He hesitates. "I hate to ask, but I'm in a desperate situation. Can I come in for a moment?"

For ultra-formal Gus to ask to come in, there must be something serious going on.

"Of course." I take the tray from him and step back, leaving space for him to enter my cabin.

Putting the tray on my table, I ask, "What's going on?"

Still he hesitates. He pulls his fancy hat off and holds it in his hand, worrying the brim of it with nervous fingers. "The thing is..." he clears his throat. "What I mean is, you're friends with Pinky, aren't you?"

"Yes."

"I think I made her angry a few weeks ago. I didn't intend to."

"What happened?" I'm aware that Pinky has never been fond of what she considers Gus's superior attitude.

"I said the wrong thing. A porter asked me to get him a drink, and I was on my way to make a report to the captain and, in my distraction, I asked him if I looked like a bartender. I didn't realize Pinky was nearby."

Oh boy. Yeah, implying that a bartender is somehow a lowly figure would definitely piss Pinky off. "I see."

Gus rushes on, "I didn't intend it as a slight. People choose to travel on this ship just for the drinks she mixes. She's a legend in the Chance Fleet. I just wasn't thinking, that's all. I have a lot of pressure on me."

He hangs his head, looking down at his hat.

"Okay," I say slowly, trying to put this together with his need to talk to me. "So what did she do?"

"I think she highjacked the elevator. I can't prove it, but all that Chance 3000 nonsense happened right after I made that comment, and hasn't gone away since. I've spent more hours than

I can count soothing agitated guests and trying to get technical support to repair the elevator. Somehow, every diagnostic comes up just fine. No tech can ever replicate the problem."

I stifle a laugh. The idea of programmer after programmer checking out the elevator and finding it perfectly operational when it's actually stopping for dance parties and moments of contemplation strikes me as funny.

Poor Gus.

"I was thinking, since you're friends and all," Gus ventures, "maybe you could talk to her for me. Help me get the elevator back to normal."

This is tricky. I'm in between two important figures who run this ship. "I promise to talk to her about it. I can't guarantee it will make any difference, though. Maybe it isn't even her."

"Maybe," Gus allows, though I can tell he doesn't believe it's a possibility. "But if you'd talk to her about it, I'd be grateful."

"Of course," I say. "I'll see what I can find out."

He bows enthusiastically. "Thank you, Mr. Kenny! You have my undying gratitude."

"Then, do you think you could call me Charlie?" I'd rather he address me informally.

But Gus looks horrified. "Like a sectarian rube? I'm sorry, sir, I simply cannot."

He stalks out of my room, chin high. He is a proud, proud man, that Gus. That's probably the attitude that got himself saddled with a dance-party elevator.

THE WEEK LEADING up to our stop on Mars is pleasantly uneventful. I get a lot of work done, watch some movies, and Pinky teaches me a couple more drink recipes.

I don't see much of Greta, though, and that's a real downside. She's occupied with her own work, and preparing for her movie role. I don't know how many ways there are to say, "Don't worry about it," but it must be a lot.

On the big day, she tells us to come to the set at noon. She's arranged passes for us and everything. She leaves a few hours before, saying they do photography and stuff beforehand, for promotional reasons.

The time crawls. I'm more eager than I expected to see the movie set. Or maybe it's just that Greta will be in the movie. I do some work, but I'm not as focused as I should be so I put it aside. I tidy my cabin, but that only takes about a minute.

I can't even go help Pinky in the bar. She's taking a day off. I might as well take a walk. The exercise is good for me.

It's rare for me to have a chance to be bored. I usually keep quite busy. I do an entire circuit around the ship, and then take a second, slower lap. Along the way, I scrutinize the ship in a way I haven't before. I admire the neat rows of identical doors, the immaculately clean deck plates, the evenness of the rivets on the bulkheads.

This is a good ship. Well-designed, pleasing to the eye, and completely comfortable. It feels like a real home to me.

Noon finally rolls around and I meet Pinky at the elevator. As we get in, I consider what Gus asked me and whether I should broach the subject now.

I wait for the Chance 3000 to start some weird crap, but it takes us down to Mars without making a sound. It's a little eerie.

We descend beneath the planet's surface and I feel a little claustrophobic. Finally, the doors open and, again, the elevator makes no sound.

"That was odd," I say as we step onto a moving sidewalk.

"It didn't do anything," Pinky answers. "How's that odd?"

"That elevator has been so strange lately. It's established a habit of it, to the point that I've come to expect it. So when it doesn't do something, that seems odd."

Pinky grunts, looking uninterested.

"You don't know anything about the elevator, do you?" I venture.

"What do you mean?"

"Well, I thought maybe it was like the poorly translated signs you have up around the ship. You know, something you'd find funny." I don't think I'm doing a good job of tackling this subject.

Pinky stares at me. "You think I could do all that to an elevator?"

"I think you can do whatever you decide to do," I answer in all honestly.

She frowns at me, but then her expression morphs into a smirk. "Good. I like that."

The moving sidewalk ends and we need to switch to another one. I move toward the one with the blue stripe along its length, according to Greta's directions.

"You sure it's not the yellow line?" Pinky points in the other direction.

"Positive. Blue line, all the way down. Then there's supposed to be someone to greet us and take us the rest of the way."

She shrugs. "All right, if you say so."

"It's definitely blue," I insist.

"I said okay. Jeez." She steps onto the blue line with the look of someone who has been nagged most heinously.

I also notice that she has sidestepped the issue of the elevator, which is suspicious. But I decide to let it drop. For now.

One line leads to another and then a young human guy meets us, as Greta promised. He ushers us to a room with lots of cameras, an overabundance of people, and a strange, charged atmosphere.

A sign is lit up with *Live Set*. A stream of people cross what looks like a street intersection on Earth. Except, of course, we're a mile below the surface on Mars.

Hooray for movie magic.

I spot Greta. She's walking along, wearing an expensive-looking suit and looking important. A tall guy bumps into her and says, "Excuse me."

Wow, we arrived at the perfect time to hear Greta deliver her line.

She looks up at the guy with a cursory smile and says, "Don't worry about it." She barely breaks her stride.

"Wait..." The guy seems stunned. "Elizabeth?" He touches her shoulder.

Greta turns, and her smile has slipped. She pulls her sunglasses down to peer over them. "Can I help you?"

"Elizabeth?" he says again.

"Do we know each other?" Greta asks.

He nods. "Yes, I'm Rob! Remember?"

She frowns, then a light of recognition dawns in her eyes. "Rob? Oh my gosh! I didn't recognize you!"

She flings herself into his arms and there they are, hugging and laughing while the crowd streams around them.

"And cut!" A tall, skinny man shouts. "Fantastic, you two! Greta, you're a natural."

The entire space erupts into a flurry of activity. I can't even see Greta because there are so many people and so much equipment moving to and fro.

Greta appears, hugging Pinky then me. "You made it! Did you see?"

"We saw," I confirm. "You were great. Like a real movie star."

"Looks like they expanded your part." Pinky observes.

Greta beams at us. "Yes! They liked the chemistry between me and the lead actor, and decided to tie me into his backstory. His long-lost love from high school. How fun is that?"

"Very cool," I say.

Pinky shrugs noncommittally.

"Want to meet him? Glen's a real pro, and a nice guy, too."

"Glen?" I ask.

"Glen Gresham, the actor I was just working with. Don't tell me you didn't recognize him."

I shrug. If he's not in robot westerns, I'm not likely to know him.

Greta makes a sound of exasperation. "He's been in lots of movies lately. He's the it-guy for romantic dramas."

"I don't watch many of those," I say carefully.

Pinky is less tactful. "Bunch of stupid kissy junk. If stuff doesn't blow up and no one gets shot, it's not a movie worth watching."

Greta deflates a little. "Oh. Well, okay. Let's just go then. Do you want to do some looking around before we go back to the ship?"

"We just got here," Pinky says. I guess that means she'd rather stay for a while.

"Actually, I feel claustrophobic down here," I say. "Why don't you two have some fun, and I'll go back on my own."

It could be risky, me traveling on my own, but I'm reluctant to make them go right back to the *Second Chance* just because I don't care for being underground.

I mean, it doesn't even make sense. Being underground is no more perilous than being on a space ship. In fact, it's far less so. But I just don't like it down here, and there's no rationalizing with the kind of fear that makes you feel like your bones are trying to get outside your skin."

"That's okay," Greta says. "I've been down here lots of times. I'll go back with you."

Pinky frowns at us. "It won't be as much fun without you two. But I'll do my best anyway."

Before we can get off the set, I hear a voice behind us. "*Who is that?*"

Must be some big star or something. We keep walking.

"*You there! The tall one! Please wait!*"

We pause, exchanging looks. Do they mean Pinky? We turn

around to see the director hurrying our way. His eyes are glued to Pinky.

"Who's your agent?" he asks.

Pinky gives him the look that Pinky reserves for people who aren't very smart. "I don't need an agent in my line of work."

The director, a fairly nondescript human with messy brown hair, blinks in puzzlement. "You're not a stunt actor?"

Pinky smirks at him. "I'm a stunt liver." Then she frowns. "Not, as in, like gizzards and stuff. I meant I live my life that way. That came out differently when I said it than it sounded in my head."

The director laughs. "Welcome to *my* line of work! Look, you'd be perfect for a movie I have coming up later this year. I'm trying to get Greta in on it, too. Would you be interested?"

Pinky shrugs. "I guess it depends on the details. Like everything else in life. I already have a job, but it could be fun. Have your people call my people."

She reaches into her back pocket, fishes out a business card, and hands it to the director. Then turns and walks away, like a total badass.

I scurry after her while Greta giggles.

We drop by a buffet. The buffets on Mars are legendary. The soup, oddly, is what gets the most adulation, but I get a taste of Martian hush puppies and I'm ruined for any other hush puppies for the rest of my life. It's amazing.

Afterward, with our bellies stuffed with hush puppies, we make our way back to the ship. I chat with Greta about who she met and how she likes the experience of being in a movie. Pinky parts ways with us when she notices a dance club.

"Was it fun being in a movie?" I ask Greta.

"At times," Greta says. "It was neat to see all these people working at creating something we only see as a finished product. I liked that part. I don't know that I'm cut out to be an actress, though. It was a lot of waiting around, and I bore easily."

"You were great, though," I say.

"Thanks. I did like the acting part. Especially when they gave me more lines."

"Be careful," I tease her as we arrive at the elevator. "If you get too famous, you might be mobbed by people everywhere we go."

She laughs. "I doubt that will happen from just a few lines at the end. But you're right, I'd hate the life of a major celebrity. So I guess I can check this experience off my list and keep looking forward to what's next."

"Like our visit to Earth?" After the glamor of all this movie stuff, my hometown might be a downer.

But she says, "Yes! I'm looking forward to seeing the places you think are worth visiting, and meeting your nana, too."

"She's not like she used to be. It's sad."

"None of us is what we used to be," she points out. "It's just life. And we keep living it until we can't anymore."

"You're right." The elevator's taking a long time. It must have been at the top when we arrived. "I'll keep that in mind. At least Nana's still around. At her age, that's something, for our family."

"Yeah!" She swats my arm in a way that, where I'm from, means, *You asshole!* But for Greta, it's just playful agreement.

I wonder if there are mental adjustments she's had to make to interact with people from Earth. Surely there are things we do that would normally mean something else to her.

I'm about to ask when the elevator doors open and a group of six *Second Chance* travelers shuffle off wordlessly, looking stunned.

Greta giggles as we board. "What do you think happened to them?"

"I don't know. I'm just hoping this thing has had its fun and will leave us alone."

I brace myself.

Going up.

Without even asking? Greta and I exchange a look, but don't

dare to speak aloud. The Chance 3000 might take it as a hostile act and retaliate.

A hundred and fifty thousand people die on Mars every day.

Is that a threat? It kind of feels like one.

Greta is not wearing a look of confidence either. She mouths *What now?* at me, but all I can do is shrug.

The average person on Mars spends six years of their life waiting in lines.

Is it...is it trying to depress us? Is this what happened to the people who were on here before us?

One in every three thousand Martian babies is stillborn. No reason has been found.

Greta's mouth drops open.

Arrived at up. Have a nice day.

"Nice day, my ass!" Greta says. She's carefully waited until we've exited the elevator before speaking. She turns and kicks the door. "Wasted lives and dead babies! You're a dickweed, Chance 3000!"

We turn back around only to see a nice family of four staring at us in shock.

Greta's eyes widen and she bolts. I bolt after her.

When we're out of earshot, she hisses, "I'm probably going to get complaints about that!"

I'm sympathetic. I really am. I'd hate for something like that to happen to me where I work. But for it to happen to Greta, who's surely never had to endure something so embarrassing, is kind of funny.

I snort.

She looks at me in surprise as we reach her cabin door. "Are you laughing at me?"

"No." I try to smother a snicker but fail, and not only laugh, but cough painfully on top of it.

I clamp my lips together and hold my hands over my stomach, trying to contain my mirth, but it doesn't work. I'm shaking, laughing, and gasping for breath.

After a moment of looking outraged, Greta giggles. She holds her hand over her mouth as she laughs. "Oh, I shouldn't be laughing…stop it!"

She swats my arm.

"You stop it." I swat her arm right back.

We laugh there in the corridor for two of the best minutes of my life. Then she swipes her hands over her eyes. "Ugh. I need to get to the showers and wash off all this movie makeup. It's not like the regular kind. This stuff seems like it's made from tar or glue or something."

I'm disappointed to part ways, but following her to the showers is a total creepo-pervert move, and I don't care that for some water-conserving species it's normal.

Since I don't want my disappointment to show, I say, "I guess I'll check in with work, make sure nothing important came up. Want to meet for dinner?"

"Sure. That'd be nice. At the bar?"

I was kind of hoping she'd offer her cabin, but I act like I totally meant the bar. "Yep. Just give me a call when you're hungry."

"Will do." She gives me a funny little salute. "Thanks for coming down to the set today. Sorry you didn't get to be there longer."

"I'm not," I admit. "It was interesting, but I don't think Mars is my kind of place, other than the hushpuppies."

She nods sympathetically. "Okay. See you later, then!"

She disappears into her cabin.

I linger for a moment, just in case she remembers something and pops right back out. She doesn't, though, so I scoot on down to my own cabin. In my book, it would also be a creepo-pervert move to stand outside her room, waiting to see her shuffling down the hall with a change of clothes and her loofah.

We have dinner that night, and it's entirely ordinary. Regular food, regular conversation. Since Pinky is still on Mars, we don't even have her unique perspective to mix things up.

But ordinary is good. Normal is really, really nice. Between the two of us, sometimes our luck skews her way, and sometimes it leans mine. But the equilibrium we have for this dinner, in all its average glory, is pretty special to me.

Afterward, she walks me back to my cabin. "This was nice. We don't even have to be doing anything special, and I still have a good time."

"I had a good time, too," I say.

We proceed to have a perfectly normal, run-of-the-mill awkward moment. I'm so flush with our ordinariness that I lean forward and give her a kiss on the cheek.

She smiles and I bask in the moment, until Gus comes hustling around the corner. When he sees us, he slows his roll and tries to be all proper.

"Is something wrong?" Greta asks.

"It's the elevator, miss. It has deeply insulted some Gvertflorians by implying that they appear to be octopi."

I grimace. I'm glad dealing with that situation is Gus's job and not mine. Gvertflorians do not have any sense of humor at all. They are dreadfully serious.

"Poor Gus," Greta says when he's out of sight. "I'm sure that won't be fun to deal with."

Funny. For once, someone is having worse luck than I am.

After Greta's gone and I'm tucked up in my cabin, I take some time to appreciate my change in fate.

13

The next three days are pleasantly mundane. Whatever happened on Mars seems to have energized Pinky. She's been particularly cheerful lately. The three of us fall back into our regular routines of fork training every other morning, breakfast together, and working during the day.

I could easily spend forty or fifty years this way.

Then we arrive at Earth, and my feet are suddenly made of lead. Earth is part of my old life, when I was never happy and I was due to die any day. I just don't have good associations with the place and I feel like going there will be begging bad redshirt luck to come find me again.

It's like a joke. Why did the redshirt return to his doom? To help his cyborg nana.

Fine. I didn't say it was a good joke. Quit judging. I'm worried for my life, here. Hahas are scarce when you're fearing a grisly death.

Maybe I should be making more progress with my phobias, but I've only had six months of this kind of life, compared to twenty-plus years living under the spectre of doom.

These things take time.

I'm using all of my self-calming techniques as I descend to the planet of my birth. I breathe deeply. I visualize my health and well-being. I calculate the odds of various possibilities. Most of all, I stick close to Pinky and Greta. They are the only way I'll make it out of this alive.

The elevator doesn't give us any shit, and for that I'm grateful. I have enough occupying my headspace right now.

Greta's been trying to teach me to look on the bright side. So, on the bright side, at least my cyborg nana is less likely to disapprove of me hanging out with a Garbdorian and a Mebdarian mutant. I think she'd have been fine with Greta even before she got assimilated, but I could see her finding Pinky unnerving. Nana lived a fairly sheltered existence as a redshirt. Until the cyborgs showed up, anyway.

We reach the bottom and the doors open. Here we are. On Earth. My old stomping grounds. The place of my birth.

The place I hadn't intended to return to.

Nana still lives in the same little house. You'd think her daily life would change a lot more after assimilation, but it isn't like that with the cyborgs. They're not raising an army or anything. They're slowly building a consensus, which will eventually become a majority. Then they'll be able to control things on a political level. It's smart, in a slow-moving, grass-roots kind of way. Since people who are assimilated are still citizens of their respective planets, they can't be deported.

All Nana really has to do, outside of her knitting and her crappy baking, is report to the cyborg union every week. She says the meetings aren't so bad, either. Cyborgs aren't much for waxing poetic or playing to the crowd. They just announce basic information and that's that.

Plus, Nana gets a monthly stipend from the cyborg union. So it's not all bad. I like knowing she has plenty of pocket money to play canasta. Even after her big change, she's a wicked canasta player. Her implants actually make her better at it, to the dismay of her card buddies. So the change hadn't been all bad for her.

I hate the idea of her suffering equipment failures, though.

We walk up the neat little stone path that leads up to her door. She used to be a good gardener, but not so much these days. Though she weeds and waters regularly, she has no eye for landscape design. She mashes plants together in one space, then leaves adjacent swathes entirely barren. And she tends to make everything way too geometric.

Not everything needs to be a sphere or a cube, Nana. These are shapes that just don't occur very often with plants.

I step up, ring Nana's doorbell, and wait.

Nothing.

I ring again. I can hear the bell inside the house, so I know it isn't broken. She said something about her acoustic processor not being right, so maybe she can't hear?

I try the door, but it's locked.

"Charlie?" A voice comes from behind me.

I turn and see Nana's neighbor. "Hello, Mrs. Dubstep. Nana's expecting me, but not answering the door."

"Yes, she left a message with me. There was an emergency canasta session, and she'd gone to it. She said to tell you she'll be back in four hours."

"An emergency card game session?" I'm unsure what would constitute such a circumstance.

Mrs. Dubstep nods.

"And it will last four hours?"

She nods again.

"Ah, okay, I guess." What else can I say? "We'll come back later."

"It's good you've come to visit. You're such a good boy." Mrs. Dubstep smiles at me. "Her hand keeps falling off, and it's driving her crazy."

My nana's hand keeps falling off, but she's off on an emergency four-hour canasta bender. Sure. That makes sense.

Mrs. Dubstep disappears back into her house, which is a mirror of Nana's cute little cottage.

I look to Greta and Pinky. "I guess that leaves us some time for sightseeing."

"Yay!" Greta hops up and down. "I want to buy a funny hat."

Is that a thing where she's from? "I'm not sure if there will be hats," I say. "I mean, maybe. Mostly we have t-shirts and water globes as souvenirs. But we can look for hats."

As soon as I say it, I feel like a putz, because if Greta wants to find a hat, she will. But she just beams at me, full of apparent excitement.

"Okay. Should we start with the Statue of Liberty? We'll need to take a train, then a ferry."

Greta hops some more. "Let's do it!"

Pinky nods, so I lead them down the lane and we catch a taxi to take us to the train.

Pinky frowns at me. "A taxi, to get to a train, so we can get on a ferry? This is inefficient."

"I know. This part of New France is like that."

"New France?" Greta looks puzzled. "I thought the Statue of Liberty was on some island near New York. I had to memorize a lot of sightseeing facts when I started with the Chance Fleet, and I'm sure I remember it."

"You're right," I assure her as we get out of the taxi and purchase train tickets at the automated kiosk. "Historically, this part of Earth was known as New York. It's part of a region that was known as the United States until recently. About fifty years ago, we struck a trade alliance with France. One stipulation of the deal was renaming the state *New France*."

"Those are the wine and cheese people, right?" Greta's face scrunches up as if pulling these facts from her brain is painful.

"Yeah, no one saw that change coming. And between you and

me, behind closed doors, we just keep on using the regular names. The renaming is just a commercial thing. It'll change back in a few years anyway, when the naming rights expire."

"Wow." Greta seems stuck between being impressed and being confused. I frequently feel the same way about it.

We walk across the train terminal to the boarding platform.

"We wait here until we get the signal for boarding to begin," I explain.

Pinky's looking at the train the way a five-year-old might. All big eyes and enthusiasm. "Think they'll let me shovel coal?"

I hate to disappoint her. "No, they haven't used coal for a few hundred years. Too messy and inefficient."

Her expression falls. "Is there anything I can shovel? I've always wanted to do some manual labor aboard mass transit."

It's a strange dream, but who am I to judge?

"I don't think so," I say gently. "But maybe you can meet the driver." Usually this privilege is limited to children, but I think in Pinky's case they'll make an exception.

"I guess it'll do," Pinky says sourly, crossing her arms over her chest.

People hustle by, carrying bags and suitcases. I'm glad we're not at the station during a peak time. I hate crowds. Already, this place has more activity than I'd prefer.

A man in a dapper hat yells in a resounding voice, "Allll aboard!"

I start forward, but Pinky and Greta keep standing there. "That's the signal to board," I say.

"What, that bellow?" Greta blinks at me.

"Yes. It's nostalgic. From the days before electronic messaging."

"Oh. Cool. I guess." Greta shrugs and follows me.

Pinky looks unimpressed. I think she's still mad about not getting to shovel coal.

"Do you think I could get a hat like the one the guy who yelled was wearing?" Greta asks.

What's with her and hats today? But I don't say anything about it. "That's the one you want?"

"Yeah. I like it. It's so...stripey." Greta nods.

"I'm sure we can find one somewhere."

"One for me, too," Pinky says. "Stripey is cool."

We board and find our seats. Greta and I sit side by side facing front, while Pinky has the opposite pair of seats to herself. She faces us, frowning. Scowling, actually. The people across the aisle have noticed and are getting nervous.

A car attendant hurries over. "Is everything okay over here?" Waves of worry seem to roll off her.

I defer to Greta so she can work her magic.

She gives the attendant a big smile and, is it just me or does she seem a little extra luminescent for just a few seconds there?

"Hi," Greta says warmly. "We were wondering if we could visit the engine car and meet the engineer at some point. It's our first trip on an Earth train." She says this last in a confiding way, which comes across as delightfully endearing.

The attendant glances from Greta to Pinky and back. I don't think I even exist at the moment, as far as she's concerned. "I'm sure that could be arranged. Welcome aboard. Is there anything else we can do to make your ride enjoyable?"

Pinky's scowl eases into a mere frown. "Do you have that drink stuff Earth is famous for?"

The attendant looks puzzled, but keeps smiling. "We might! Do you know the name of it?"

"I've heard it's yellow and sour like battery acid." Pinky looks hopeful.

The attendant has no response to that. She just keeps smiling bravely.

"Pinky, do you mean lemonade?" I ask.

"That's the one!" Pinky nods.

How is a bartender unfamiliar with lemonade? If it were anyone else, I might suspect some sectarian rube-ishness at play.

The attendant nods. "Of course! Shall I bring three lemonades while I send word to the engineer?"

"That'd be sporting of you," Pinky says approvingly.

The poor woman looks so relieved that I feel sorry for her, and she hurries off to score some lemonade.

I peek at the people across the aisle. They keep giving us furtive looks, but don't seem as anxious as before.

Twenty minutes later we're sipping lemonade, watching the landscape fly by the window, and waiting for the engineer to call us up. I don't really want to visit the engine. I don't hate trains or anything, I just don't need to visit the place where the driving happens.

When the attendant returns to let us know we can go back to the engine, I opt to remain. "You two go have a look. I'll stay here."

"You sure?" Greta asks. "I could stay here if you'd rather."

"No, go ahead." Pinky's already on her way, so I whisper, "Just keep Pinky out of trouble."

She giggles and nods before hurrying off after our tall friend.

They remain absent for the rest of the ride. I don't mind. With the gentle rocking of the train, I could almost fall asleep. But I won't. Because falling asleep in public is a great way for a guy like me to get robbed, beaten, or wake up in a tub of ice in Hoboken with both my kidneys missing.

Not today, organ pirates!

The train has stopped and the other passengers have disembarked by the time Pinky and Greta finally return. Improbably, they're both wearing train conductor hats and looking quite pleased about it.

I say nothing.

I continue to say nothing on the ferry ride, and by the time we finally step out and get a good view of the Statue of Liberty, I've kind of forgotten about the hats.

We stand looking at the big green metal majesty of the statue. Pinky nods slowly. "I like it. She looks like someone I could be friends with. Do you think I could get a pointy hat like hers?"

A big, metal crown with huge spikes? I doubt it. But I say, "Hm, I don't know. Might be tough."

"A shame. Everyone should have one of those. Maybe I'll get one custom-made. I know a guy."

I feel a strange sense of synchronicity. Somehow, Pinky fits in Old New York/New France better than I ever did. She does it without even trying, too.

We wander around, eat some funnel cake, and just kind of waste time until we can get back to Nana's house. It's nice. It makes me think of how I would have misspent my youth if I'd had the chance.

Better late than never.

The trip back to Nana's is easier going. My friends are already champs at taking the ferry and the train, and though Pinky complains again about the taxi, we return to Nana's in good spirits.

I ring the doorbell and almost immediately the door opens. Nana steps out of the house.

Back in her day, Nana was a bonafide beauty. She's pretty even now, with the left side of her face covered in cybernetics. She always said her left eye was a little lower than her right anyway. Now it doesn't matter. She has a carefully coiffed puff of thick white hair, done up in an old-world style of wavy glamor. Most of her body below her chin is hardware. It's good that it cured her arthritis, but bad that she can't get repairs when she needs them. She wears a feminine dress in some old-lady style, with lacy stuff around the edges.

"Charlie. Come give your nana a hug." Her voice has a metallic ring, but it mostly sounds like her.

I give her a hug, careful not to dislodge any hoses or scrape myself on metal.

"I'm so glad you came. Who are these people?"

"Greta and Pinky." I point to them in turn. "The best friends in the universe."

"I didn't think I'd live to see the day," Nana says. "But then, I didn't think I'd have an exhaust hose instead of a rectum, so there you go."

Greta laughs in surprise, but Pinky nods approvingly. "I like her."

Nana didn't used to be so blunt, but now that I see Pinky digging it, it occurs to me that the two of them have things in common. Huh. I wonder if that has something to do with my nearly instant liking of Pinky.

"You've done well." Nana's looking at my friends. "You should marry her. You'd have cute babies."

Even cyborg nanas worry about marrying off their grandkids.

"Which one?" I ask, wondering if she can pick up on my love for Greta.

"Either. They're both good. I can tell." Nana tilts her head to one side. "Though, I doubt you could handle the big one. Sexually speaking."

"You got that right," Pinky agrees.

You probably think I'm dying a thousand deaths of embarrassment, but actually I'm not. Sure, my nana and my friend are talking about my sexual prowess, and right in front of the woman I love, too, but I long ago gave up the idea that I even had any sexual prowess. So nope. I have no feelings to hurt in that regard.

Besides, I agree with them.

"Come in, I'm making tea." Nana doesn't wait for an answer. She just goes into the house and leaves us to follow.

As we enter, she greets Greta and Pinky as if they were guests going through a receiving line at a wedding. She clasps their hands and thanks them for coming. "You can call me Rose. Or Nana, like Charlie does."

"You got it, Nana Rose." Pinky points at Nana and makes a loud click sound with her tongue.

We sit at Nana's little table in the kitchen and she fusses with cups and saucers and pouring tea. When I take a sip, I'm relieved to find that it's not bad tea. It's thoroughly tolerable.

Then she breaks out the cookies. "I almost forgot these," she says as she arranges them daintily on a plate. "They're Charlie's favorite."

I try to warn my friends with my eyes, but it's tough to convey panic and destruction without Nana also seeing it.

Greta takes a polite nibble, smiles, and sets the cookie down under the guise of sipping her tea. She's clever like that.

Pinky's chewing thoughtfully after tossing a whole cookie into her mouth. "Minty. I like it."

Oatmeal cookies are not supposed to be minty. But, because I love Nana, I take a bite and chew, smiling as if hell demons of doom are not dancing on my taste buds.

What is that other flavor? It's kind of…grassy. And then there's the weird taste that is both metallic and oily, and seems to be the signature flavor of all her baking.

"I added some green tea leaves, to make them fancy," Nana adds.

This is not what fancy tastes like. But I smile at Nana all the same, while formulating a plan to dispose of the cookie when she's not looking.

If I talk, I can't eat. "So, Nana. What's the problem you're having with unrepaired parts?"

"My joints all need to be realigned and tightened. My hearing is not right. And my shoulder has a tendency to hitch at the most inopportune times." Nana rubs her right shoulder.

"Mrs. Dubstep said your hand keeps falling off," I say.

"Oh, that busybody. I wasn't going to mention that. Don't want to seem like a complainer." Nana pouts.

"Nobody thinks that," Greta assures her. "You deserve to get the maintenance you need. We'll make sure you do."

"It won't be easy," Nana warns. "The cyborg union is notoriously chintzy when it comes to repairs. You pretty much have to have an entire system failure for them to do anything."

"Not cool," Pinky says after swallowing another cookie. I think she actually likes them, and that makes me question things about her. "Greta's right. We'll make sure you get what you need."

"Hot damn, I'll be swimming in oil tonight!" Nana rubs her hands together.

Nana always liked the phrase "hot damn" but the idea of swimming around in oil only became an appealing one to her after being assimilated.

She takes off her apron, hangs it on a peg, and smooths her dress. Then she stands by the door. "Well?"

Oh. She wants to leave *now*.

We jump up and follow Nana.

"You got it, Nana Rose," Pinky says on the way to Nana's car. "Let's go make those bastards fix your hand, and the rest of you, too."

"Damn straight." Nana holds up her metal fist and Pinky fist bumps it.

What's happening here? Greta and I exchange a look of uncertainty.

Pinky has apparently won front-seat privileges, because Nana tells me to sit in the back with Greta. Or maybe she's still working the marriage angle. It's hard to tell with her.

Nana was an iffy driver back in the day when she was entirely biological. Now, she's a downright terrifying one. She calculates things so precisely that she can drive in a way that, for anyone else, would be insanely reckless.

It doesn't help that every time our bodies get crushed down

with g-force thanks to a sharp turn, Pinky raises her hands and yells, "Whooo, that's it, Nana Rose! Metal to the pedal!"

The first time this happens, Greta says, "Isn't it pedal to the metal?"

"Nah," Pinky says, pointing at Nana. "Cyborg."

I laugh. Greta laughs. Then Nana takes another sharp turn and I feel like I might lose my tea.

In no time at all, we pull up to the cyborg union office. It occurs to me at this point that we haven't come up with any specific plan. We're showing up with nothing but the desire to help Nana.

Well, we also have Greta's luck. And everything that Pinky brings to the table.

So, yeah. We're good. We got this.

We get out of that car gangsta-style. I wish I could film it, because it's like a movie. Nana and Pinky lead, with Greta and me flanking them. We walk side by side right up to the door like a group of highly intimidating vigilantes. I imagine what we would look like in slow-mo.

Nana opens the door and the moment is ruined because we have to line up single file to enter, and that's just too orderly to be cool anymore.

But we're in now, and those cyborgs are going to get an earful. Well, if they have ears. Okay, let's just say they're going to have their asses handed to them. Wait. Same problem.

Damn, why do so many phrases for throwing down involve body parts?

Whatever. We strut right up and…take a number. Because there's no one here. Just a number-ticket machine. Apparently this place is entirely automated.

Of course. Because cyborgs.

We are so screwed once cyborgs compose the majority of the population.

We sit down on the hard, uncomfortable chairs and wait. Even Pinky cannot make sitting in a waiting room look cool.

Even though no one else is in the room, it takes a good fifteen minutes for the sign on the door to change to *Now serving number twenty-eight*. A latch mechanism in the door pops.

Pinky stands up.

"We're twenty-nine, dear," Nana says, waving her ticket.

"Well, today, we're twenty-eight." Pinky opens the door.

Yeah, she's got her cool back. I don't know if it comes across to you while you're reading this, but it's the way she said it that matters. She sounded like Zorbo Blergbot in the movie *Laserfight in the DNS Corral*. All tough and gritty and stuff, like she eats steel beams and spits them out.

On second thought, maybe she does.

We follow Pinky's lead and enter a room with cyborgs sitting at teller windows. One window is labeled *Employment*. That's not the one. The second has a sign that says *Referrals* and I don't want to think too hard about what that means. The third says *Maintenance*, which seems like the place for us.

There's only one chair opposite the teller, so we encourage Nana to sit. She's probably tougher than any of us, but it seems like the right thing to do for an old lady.

"Can I help you?" the teller asks.

"I've sent a dozen requisition forms, but I haven't been able to get repairs. I need joint maintenance. Especially for my hand." Nana holds out the faulty extremity, palm up.

"You look functional," the teller says, scrutinizing Nana.

"Well I'm not falling over or unable to activate my circuits, but is that what it takes to get service?" Nana asks.

"If we give everyone free tweaks that they don't really need, how will we have time to service the people who really need it?" the teller reasons.

"I don't know, maybe you let the people who are struggling decide if they really need it? Aren't they the best judge of that?"

"No." The teller sits straighter, and I can tell she's about to refuse to help Nana.

"Look," I say. Everyone looks at me. Uh oh. I didn't have a good speech planned or anything. I'm just going off the cuff. This doesn't bode well. "You cyborgs go around assimilating people and then not living up to your obligations. Nana didn't ask to be assimilated. You did that. If you don't start stepping up and helping people who ask for it, I'll..." My mind races for a threat. I mean, what can I really do about it? What can anyone do? If cyborgs were easy to thwart, we'd have found a way to keep them from assimilating poor old nanas in their own kitchens.

My gaze goes to Greta. Greta of the golden glow and the woman I love, who has all the luck. How far can I push that luck?

Let's see.

"I'll call the Gvertflorian prime minister and ask his people to rid Earth of cyborgs once and for all."

Everyone knows that Gvertflorians have a blood feud with cyborgs. Dang, there's the body-part issue coming up again. Can you have a blood feud with cyborgs? They don't have much blood. Maybe they have an oil feud or a coolant feud or something.

Urg.

Anyway, Gvertflorians hate cyborgs and would be delighted to come rain hell upon them. That'll never happen because the fallout would be tremendous and Earthers aren't about to sign up for that.

The teller clearly doesn't believe me. She shouldn't either. It's a ridiculous claim. Here's where I back up my claim with some fake proof. I hope.

I hand my telcoder to Greta. "Call the prime minister's office and tell them we may need to call in that favor."

Greta gives me a look of panic, but she takes the telcoder and begins punching in numbers. A lot of numbers. Like, fifty of them. Intergalactic calling is a nightmare.

She turns her head, so only Pinky and I can see her look of surprise. "Oh! Yes, please hold one moment."

She hands the telcoder to me.

I hand it to the teller. "Here. This is the prime minister's private secretary. Heed my warning: you will be thinking about whatever happens next for the rest of your life. Don't make it something you'll regret."

The teller looks unsure. She takes the telcoder. "Hello?"

The servo on her neck makes a popping sound. She thrusts the telcoder at me. "Take it!" she hisses.

I say into it, "Please stand by," as if there is something to stand by for. Then I fix the cyborg with a look.

She backs away. "I'll arrange Rose's repairs immediately. I will also call an emergency union meeting with all representatives. We wish to avoid a Gvertflorian conflict."

"Yeah, ya do," Pinky drawls. "Get your robot ass moving. Nana Rose needs fixing."

When the teller leaves through the back, I want to sag into a chair, but there isn't one. I will my bones to remain solid for at least a little while longer. I lean against the wall and let out a long breath.

Oh no, the telcoder. I put it to my ear, and the line is still open. Crap. "Apologies," I say. "We'll call back later."

Pinky, Greta, Nana, and I are trying to contain ourselves. We're well aware that there are probably listening devices, and maybe video monitoring, too. Though I have a strong desire to cheer and celebrate our success, I hold it all in.

A cyborg man wearing a white coat enters. "Hello, Mrs. White. I hear you're having joint issues? If you'll come with me, we'll get those fixed right now."

He leads Nana away, and the teller returns.

Pinky leans toward her. "If we have to come here again, I'm not going to be nearly so nice. And I'll be looking for you, personally. Got it?"

The teller's neck servo makes another popping sound. "I assure you, the issue has already been handled. This won't happen again."

"Make sure it doesn't. I like punching stuff."

She walks back toward the waiting room.

"She really does," Greta says before following.

I feel like I should leave some last, parting words. Something really cool like Zorbo Blergbot would say.

Nothing comes to me. It seems I've used up all of my cleverness for the day. I just point at her menacingly, then follow my friends.

We go right past the waiting room and outside the building. Once in the outdoors, I feel like I can breathe again. That building was downright oppressive.

Greta, Pinky, and I cheer, hug one another, do some funky victory dance moves, and generally make people either stare or turn around and walk the other direction.

We're so hyped up on our success that I send Nana a message that we're going to do some window shopping while we wait. I don't know how long cyborg maintenance takes, but I'm guessing she's going to get the extra-uber deluxe treatment, so I figure we have time to kill.

The first shop is a jewelry store, and while I'd like to do the cute shopping-for-a-ring thing with Greta, that experience is way off in the distant future. Maybe. I hope.

We skip the jewelry store. We also have no need for the beef jerky store. Why is there a whole store for that? It defies explanation.

The third store is a winner. It's a monument and sculpture store, but Pinky spots something and strides right in.

With surprisingly little resistance, although with a hearty helping of puzzlement, the man inside removes a metal crown from a sculpture.

"But what are you..." he begins as he hands it to Pinky.

She puts the Statue of Liberty crown on her head. I must admit, it looks rather regal on her.

She looks to me for an opinion.

"Majestic," I say.

"Magnificent," Greta adds.

Pinky looks to the man, who looks taken aback.

"Uh...dignified?" he offers.

Pinky nods approvingly. "I'll take it. How much?"

The man says, "It's really not meant to be an individual..." he sighs and shakes his head. "How's two hundred?"

"Sold," Pinky declares as if he'd been plying her with his wares.

He rings up the sale. Being the professional he is, he asks, "Would you like a box for it?"

"No thanks, mate. I'll wear it out."

We do some more window shopping before going back to meet Nana. We find nothing else of interest, but it doesn't matter. Nothing could have topped Pinky's find.

WE ARRIVE BACK at Nana's house in a wave of triumph and satisfaction. We troop into her little cottage and she embarrassingly regales us with stories of my childhood.

Even cyborg nanas are biologically required to engage in this rite of passage.

Pinky wears her glorious crown the whole time. Instead of objecting to her wearing a hat in the house, Nana wholeheartedly approves. She and Pinky have so much in common, it's spooky.

Meanwhile, Greta hugs my arm while she laughs about the time I narrowly avoided a kidnapping by a man who turned out to be a serial killer.

Yeah, I know. It sounds dark. But the way Nana tells it, it's a hoot. She's got a knack for storytelling and a certain comedic timing. I hadn't previously realized this about her.

But Greta's hugging my arm and laughing and I can feel her heartbeat and some other, softer things against my elbow, and I don't give a damn about anything else. So I laugh, too.

All too soon, it's time to leave. The *Second Chance* will be moving on, and we must move on with it. I'm sad. I feel like I'm just getting to know this version of my grandmother. But my new home is in space, and a starship waits for no man, woman, unspecified, or Nana.

It is a rule of the universe.

Nana seems sad, too. "What's your next port?" she asks.

"First, Earth's international space station, and then on for a tour of the Alpha Centauri system," Greta says.

She always knows what's ahead. She's a good brand ambassador.

"Do you think there are any tickets left?" Nana asks as she removes her apron. She's served us another round of tea and horrible cookies. At least this time, I'm able to shunt all my cookies Pinky's way, and she wolfs them down like a starving Labrador.

The Labrador species of people, not the Earth variety of dog. I'd never compare Pinky to a dog. She's far too majestic with that crown of hers.

Hell, she's majestic even without it.

"I'd have to check to be sure, but I believe so. It's rare that we're booked solid." Greta answers.

"Could you get a ticket for me, dear? Just around the Alpha Centauri system, then back to Earth again. I'd like a chance to do some traveling while I'm in good working order, and to spend time with Charlie and his friends." Nana hangs her apron on its peg and smooths it.

Greta's eyes cut to me, frantically asking if this is okay.

"It would be great to have you aboard, Nana," I say. "Greta and Pinky are the best galactic tour guides in all the solar systems."

Greta beams. Both from her happy smile and a slight increase in luminescence. It's always easy to see when Greta's happy. "Absolutely! I'll do it right now."

Greta pulls out her telcoder and, after several long moments, she announces, "Done. And, as luck would have it, I was able to get you a free room. I get comps through my employer on voyages that aren't sold out."

Nana leans forward and gently pinches her cheek. "You, my dear, are a peach." She turns to me. "You be nice to this girl, or I'll never forgive you."

Pinky saves me from having to respond to this. "Greta's not a peach. *I'm* a peach. I'll show you things in Alpha Centauri that will make your servos short out."

"Well," I say, "not actually short out. Right?"

Pinky snorts. "Not literally. But almost."

I feel like we've gotten into a weird territory. To distract, I say, "Do you need help packing, Nana?"

Nana doesn't answer. She leaves the room and comes back a moment later with a suitcase. "Nope. All cyborgs are required to be ready to evacuate at any moment. Union rules."

Right. Okay. This should be interesting.

14

Back aboard the *Second Chance*, I've gotten Nana settled into her cabin. It's across the ship from my cabin, but maybe that's okay. Gus will be looking out for her, and I can get over there in just a few minutes if I hurry. Plus, it leaves me some room for romantic freedom.

You know, just in case I need it.

Cyborg or not, Nana still goes to bed at eight o'clock in the evening. With her comfortably dozing, I join Greta and Pinky in the bar for a drink.

I arrive and, as is our custom, wait for Pinky to tell me what I'll be drinking. She likes to choose for people, and she's usually bang on.

"Cheerful Seagull," she announces, pointing at me with an accusing finger that, in other circumstances, would vex me greatly.

"Isn't that a morning drink?" Last I knew, she was only serving them as a breakfast aperitif. But Pinky makes her own rules and changes them often, so there's no telling.

"Most of the time. It's what you need right now." She spins

away to perform her violent ballet of drink making, then sets a glass in front of me.

Greta's already sipping a Thunderstorm, which is an old favorite of hers. It's what she had the first day we met, now that I think about it.

I sip my Cheerful Seagull with appreciation. Pinky's perfected the recipe, and it does, indeed, suit my mood. It has just the right mix of carbonated effervescence and acidic juice.

"Are you really okay with Nana Rose being aboard?" Pinky asks. "I'd feel weird about having my grandma along."

"Yeah. It's nice, actually. I've changed, she's changed, and it's good that we have a chance to get to know each other again."

"That's so nice." Greta looks so happy, I try extra hard to ignore the carnage of her lushfruit muffin.

Someday, I'll ask her about it. Just like someday, I'll wear that red shirt and show it who's boss.

But not today.

Today, I'm just glad to be here with my friends and my nana, looking forward to some new adventures.

I lift my glass. "To the future."

Just to be clear, this is not a normal toast for my people.

Greta clicks her glass to mine, and Pinky grabs a tall, skinny cylinder so she can join in. The glass is empty, but her sentiment is not.

"To the future," Pinky and Greta repeat, in unison.

To the future, I say again to myself. *May it be full of adventure and happiness.* I look at Greta's honest, open face, and add another private thought. *And love.*

ABOUT THE AUTHOR

Zen DiPietro is a lifelong bookworm, dreamer, and writer. Perhaps most importantly, a Browncoat Trekkie Whovian. Also red-haired, left-handed, and a vegetarian geek. Absolutely terrible at conforming. A recovering gamer, but we won't talk about that. Particular loves include badass heroines, British accents, and the smell of Band-Aids.

www.ZenDiPietro.com

OTHER WORKS

Dodging Fate Series
Dodging Fate 2: Extra Fateful, Uber Dodgy

Dragonfire Station Original Series
Dragonfire Station Book 1: Translucid
Dragonfire Station Book 2: Fragments
Dragonfire Station Book 3: Coalescence

Intersections (Dragonfire Station Short Stories)

Mercenary Warfare series
Selling Out
Blood Money
Hell to Pay
Calculated Risk
Going for Broke

Chains of Command
New Blood

Blood and Bone
Cut to the Bone
Out for Blood

To get updates on new releases and sales, sign up for Zen's newsletter.

Printed in Dunstable, United Kingdom